VELVET STUDIES

VELVET STUDIES

by

C. V. WEDGWOOD

If you fear to hurt your tender hands with
thornie school-questions there is no danger
in meddling with history which is a velvet
study and recreation work.

THOMAS FULLER
Holy Warre: Epistle Dedicatory

JONATHAN CAPE
THIRTY BEDFORD SQUARE
LONDON

FIRST PUBLISHED NOVEMBER 1946
SECOND IMPRESSION JANUARY 1948
THIRD IMPRESSION 1949

PRINTED IN GREAT BRITAIN IN THE CITY OF OXFORD
AT THE ALDEN PRESS
BOUND BY A. W. BAIN & CO. LTD., LONDON

CONTENTS

ACKNOWLEDGMENTS

My thanks are due to the editors of *The Geographical Magazine*, *Penguin New Writing*, the *Spectator*, the *Tablet*, *The Times Literary Supplement* and *Windmill* for permission to reprint eight of the following articles. With the exception of 'The Velvet Study', which has not previously been published, the remaining material in this book appeared first in *Time and Tide* to the editor of which my especial thanks are due.

C. V. W.

To

EDITH MARY FLAVELL

THE VELVET STUDY

IF I was not born a historian I was an aspirant at six and a practitioner at twelve. 'Nothing that is paper can scape me when I have time to write and tis to you', wrote Dorothy Osborne to William Temple. I needed no object and I made my own time. Nothing that was paper could scape me even though the physical labour of writing opposed a frustrating barrier between me and my goal, and the mind had five acts complete before the pencil (blunt at one end and chewed at the other) had got further than *Dramatis Personae* copied from the front of a Temple Shakespeare.

Dramatis Personae, or as I learnt to put later, *Characters in order of appearance* — the first inspiration was evidently dramatic though the taste for history had come earlier. It began presumably with the shiny picture on rollers like a map which, in the echoing playroom at my grandmother's house, presented to my unrecognizing eye Caradoc before Caesar, captive but unbowed. Not until my first history lesson was the remembered picture suddenly clothed with meaning. I was six; a world of inexhaustible possibilities opened before me — real people, real things that had really happened to them. Britons, Romans, an invasion, people with the most complicated names. I remembered them all; as soon have forgotten the names of my neighbours in class. The walk home that afternoon, up the tree-lined Kensington streets, was too short. With difficulty I compressed into it for my companion's benefit the substance of Caradoc's interesting fate, 'So he said to Caesar: Why did you want to invade us? and Caesar said . . .' But the Yale key was already in the lock and upstairs in the nursery tea was on the table and it was 'Run along and wash your hands'. Only some weeks later when I instituted a brief oral examination of the term's work did I find to my dismay that I had been talking all the while to unlistening ears.

It was an early lesson in the difficulty of imparting even the most interesting information.

Writing did not come until a year or two later, and then for a time the spell of imaginary characters was greater than that of real ones. There was my first theatre: the tiered immense semi-circle of darkness, the sudden, noiseless lifting of the curtain, and there against a mist-blue distance, lovelier than anything eye had seen or heart imagined, was a beautiful and evidently shipwrecked lady asking a group of pirates — but perhaps they weren't pirates — 'What should I do in Illyria?' From that charmed frame of light wherein they moved, the starry language flowed over me, meaningless as stars and as beautiful. It seemed reasonable on getting home to start in at once, between cocoa and bedtime, to write like Shakespeare.

In the end only the stage directions were like Shakespeare. I copied them faithfully. The failure did not greatly disconcert me. Shakespeare was acknowledged to be without an equal and I was young. Double figures lay all ahead. Meanwhile there were other impressions cramming and tumbling into my mind: Shelley and Herrick and Coleridge, *The Little Duke*, *The Pilgrim's Progress* and *Pinocchio*, and with these, unsorted and unclassified, from sources of every kind, a heroic multitude from epic and saga and ballad, fairy-tale and folk-lore: Roland and Achilles, Guy of Warwick and Lohengrin, Galahad and the Red Cross Knight, Beowulf, Theseus, and the Thrice-wise Helena, the Percy and the Douglas (and like Sir Philip Sidney, I too found my heart moved more than with a trumpet). There were handsome books with gilded tops and coloured plates, there were squat little books 'told to the children', forbidding books of unrelieved print and wonderful French picture-books, Job's Napoleon on the bridge at Lodi and Boutet de Monvel's pale Joan of Arc.

Not books only, but the cool splendours of the National Gallery, Raphael's shapely virgins, the flame glow of Rubens and the mysterious darknesses of Zurbaran's Franciscan. There were the culminating glories of the Diaghilev Ballet, with Tamar waving her rose-red scarf and the Fire-bird darting, brilliant, beneath the tree with the golden fruit, and the Swan Princess parting by moonlight from her handsome lover. One afternoon a man in a black frock-coat came sidling on between the dancers and said: 'Ladies and Gentlemen, the peace treaty has been signed.' After that there was a procession with generals on horses and a great number of royal tournaments.

Looking back now it is possible to analyse the peculiar dualism of childhood. One part of the mind stored these over-violent impressions to release them suddenly in fiery inspiration or panic fear, for the Baba Yaga came crackling through the Chiltern beechwoods, the dreadful northern stalo creaked and whispered among the London planes, Clerk Saunders's ghost followed me on the stairs and Prince Lucifer himself sometimes lurked under the bed. But at other times an unwritten masterpiece flashed all-glorious through my brain and the blunt stumblings of the pencil no longer mattered.

Yet alongside these moments of dazzling and fearful imagination, there were the agitated sortings and classifyings of a painfully industrious mind. And since the fears and the imaginings were less evident than the albums of old masters and the charts of dates it was as an unimaginative child with a memory for facts that my elders saw me. Certainly there were long periods, as I grew older, during which the strain of classifying, dating and placing the artist, the school, the style of poem or picture prevented all spontaneous enjoyment. Yet though the arts came thus, for some years, to be drained of pleasure, the past never lost its enchantment. A cross, difficult, lumpish child, I felt more at home in it than in the present. Among the friendly dead, being bad at games did not seem to matter.

New shapes and patterns gradually emerged. The disjointed procession of kings and statesmen spaced along the years assumed in perspective interesting formations. They were linked in chains of progress or movement, fascinating to follow as the pencil line which on the puzzle page of *The Rainbow* (my secret vice) could be drawn from dot No. 1 to dot No. 56 until there, complete, was a duck or a rabbit. Behind these emerging arabesques of development the jumbled backgrounds fell into place, poetry, pictures and cathedrals, and more remotely conceived, but quite clear even to me, an enormous population of nameless human beings.

The perception of form in history gave me I suppose the first discoverer's excitement. I caught it once again with all its old enchantment, when I found in Maitland the whole architecture of a period built up from the analysis of its detail. It is the excitement which comes again, sudden and spasmodic, at those rewarding moments when – after long study – the logic of an incomprehensible situation suddenly becomes clear. With this discovery of form in history came the parallel recognition that truth has more than one face.

Three things after that: all together, or at least so close as to make their chronology too hard to disentangle: my father's sobering advice on writing, my discovery of documentary evidence and the *Decline and Fall of the Roman Empire*.

By the time I was twelve my writing had grown dangerously swift. There was a special kind of writing pad called 'The Mammoth', two hundred pages, quarto, ruled feint; under my now practised pencil Mammoths disappeared in a twinkling. 'You should write history,' my father said, hoping to put on a brake. 'Even a bad writer may be a useful historian.' It was damping, but it was sense. It was, after all, unlikely that I would ever be Shakespeare.

Soon after came the electrifying discovery of the document. My temperament being neither scientific nor inquiring I had not given much thought to the sources of the historical information which I acquired. One day at school our teacher read us letters to illustrate a lesson, and a fragment of a diary. The immense revelation dazzled me. Here was direct knowledge for the asking. Immediate contact could be made with these dead, so distant yet to me so tantalizingly near. After that, certain of my goal but uninstructed how to reach it, I breathed for hours on the show cases of the British Museum copying out all the documents on view. I ransacked the historical tomes of my father's library for anything between inverted commas. I found Pepys of course and was puzzled and rather shocked, Clarendon and was swept out of my depth, the Verney papers and regained my footing.

Whether it is that I have never quite outgrown the first excitement of that discovery, I find in myself to this day an unwillingness to read the secondary authorities which I have difficulty in overcoming. Indeed it is rather the fear of some learned reviewer's 'the author appears to be ignorant of the important conclusions drawn by Dr. Stumpfnadel' — than a desire to know those conclusions for their own sake which, at the latter end of my own researches, drives me to consult the later authorities.

Yet there was at this time a more subtle influence at work of which the documents were but one outward sign. Certainly I could name the hour and the place of my starting-point on the long road I have followed since: it was a small class-room on the topmost floor of a majestic stuccoed house in Kensington. Out of the windows, far below, the traffic passed up and down the tree-lined street like clock-work. It must have been summer for the trees were in leaf and the sun was shining. The class-room was painted dark green and white; at one end there was a picture of William III landing at Torbay and at the other of Wolfe scaling the Heights of Abraham. It was here that I found, in the witty, determined grey-haired lady, who dominated the scene from behind a very large desk on a very small rectangular platform, the teacher who knew how to unlock the sluice gates between the arid flats of my intellect and the flood-waters of my imagination. The desert burgeoned; the Mammoth pads flowered into an enormous History of England.

Almost immediately afterwards came Gibbon, an imposing birthday present, half a challenge. I got down to it at once, ostentatiously out of bravado, but went on out of insistent passion, evening after evening, in the yellow nursery light. 'Understandest thou what thou readest?' my grandfather mocked. I understood this much: that here was a master, here was material shaped and subdued, men and centuries brought into order, a whole world frozen in the sharp, dispassionate light of a single mind. Before this immense achievement I stood amazed, almost, for the first time, humbled. But certain: this was the star for my wagon.

At twelve I had no theory of history. Since then I have had many, even for some years the theory that in the interests of scholarship it is wrong to write history comprehensible to the ordinary reader, since all history so written must necessarily be modified and therefore incorrect. This was I think always too much against my nature to have held me long.

Acquaintance with the work of foreign historians sharpened my consciousness of the different angles from which the same events may be viewed. The associations of places, the evidence of ballad and tradition, the 'accepted' errors revealed to me little by little the delicate embroidery which can be wrought by legend on fact, embroidery which may have value as well as beauty, since it may reveal a significance in the fact not apparent from the fact itself. My own varying estimates of the facts themselves, as the years passed, showed me too clearly how much of history must always rest in the eye of the beholder; our deductions are so often different it is impossible they should always be right.

Reading Bacon's *Novum Organum* I recognize in middle life how much I am a Platonist, how given up to the doctrine of acatalepsy. For the whole value of the study of history is for me its delightful undermining of certainty, its cumulative insistence of the differences of point of view. But a writer greater than I can ever hope to be and a better historian than many historians will allow[1] has said that to write history three things are necessary: 'a capacity for absorbing facts, a capacity for stating them, and a point of view'. But what point of view can emerge from the deliberate multiplication of points of view? It is therefore in search of an ultimate point of view that I am now pursuing my velvet study back to its source.

If poetry and colour and shape have all been important to me, it is evidently in that initial *Dramatis Personae* that the ultimate reason lies. For human life is essentially dramatic; it is born and exists in conflict, conflict between men, conflict between men and circumstances, or conflict within the confines of a single human skull. This conflict is the core of every development in time. It is this conflict with which all life is bound up and on which is poised the whole powerful and awful potentiality of human endeavour. In the individual conflict lies the first reason for those mysterious abstracts, economic trends and social movements, which in our text-books are apt to become disembodied concepts. The individual — stupendous and beautiful paradox — is at once infinitesimal dust and the cause of all things.

The danger of this point of view for the practising historian is evident. The selective winnowing of time leaves only a few recognizable individuals behind for the historian to light on. Thus the historian who finds the human being more interesting than what the human being has done must inevitably endow the comparatively few individuals he can identify with too great an importance in relation to their time. Even so, I prefer this over-estimate to the opposite method which treats developments as though they were the massive anonymous waves of an inhuman sea or pulverizes the fallible surviving records of human life into the grey dust of statistics.

The human mind is too vast in all its activities for one mind to master. The attempt, foredoomed to failure, must yet be made.

[1] Lytton Strachey who has suffered from imitators who have neither his learning nor his style and who mistake a kind of vulgar derisiveness for the delicately percipient malice of the master.

Not to understand is to admit defeat. Nothing is outside the province of the historian however much may be outside his personal scope. Prejudice is a failure of the understanding, and lack of prejudice may safely be aimed at, for it will not be achieved. In any case, it is not lack of prejudice which makes for dull history, but lack of passion.

The human mind, in all its baffling strangeness and variety, is yet to be charted. One common humanity can produce a Napoleon and a Buddha, the guards at Buchenwald and the nuns of Leper Island. This immense contradiction is the historian's province; he has all the past to practise on and all the time that is left to us to solve the problem.

Or has he? For in the end he is only another ant industriously working away at his own particular conflict in the gigantic, indifferent ant-heap. When the megalomania which Mr. E. M. Forster believes, not without justification, to be the occupational disease of historians begins to affect me, I hear the voice of the royal layman apostrophizing England's greatest historian: 'Another damned thick square book! Always scribble, scribble, scribble! Eh, Mr. Gibbon?' That at least is a salutary reminder of the deafness of the world. To check other vanities and other ambitions there is the measured dictum of England's second greatest historian that to be great in this profession is perhaps 'the rarest of intellectual distinctions'.

CAVALIER POETRY AND CAVALIER POLITICS[1]

THE restlessness of the seventeenth century is a massive restlessness, reflected in gigantic convolutions of stone and tempestuous statuary. In Western Europe this was perhaps the most unhappy century until our own time, and it is closer to our own than any other in the causes of that unhappiness. Between the joyous experimentalism of the sixteenth century and the intellectual serenity of the eighteenth, it interposes a period of bewilderment: a time (like ours) in which man's activities had outrun his powers of control.

The change from a land to a money basis for society, and the conflict between State and individual were important elements in the unrest of the time, but they were not its fundamental cause, while the apparent struggle between Catholic and Protestant was a mere pendant of political issues. A mental conflict stronger than the material quarrels which set Europe's entangled dynasties and growing nations against each other divided the mind of the individual against itself: the struggle between reason and revelation.

Mysteriously, slowly, the planets, in the sixteenth century, were seen to move. The solar system became apparent through the eyes of Copernicus. When Galileo, in the early seventeenth century, set the world itself spinning, the Holy Office stepped in; too late. Only a few years afterwards William Harvey discovered a yet more intimate circulation, that of the blood in the human body. The static world dissolved in motion.

But at the beginning of the seventeenth century, the ordinary educated man lived, as he had lived for the past thousand years, by revelation. The daytime of the faith was over, but the sun

[1] *Penguin New Writing*, 21.

had not set: far and fading, it was still the light men knew. Saint Teresa was newly dead and very newly canonized. Men had seen miracles and were to see them for some years more. The curtains had not yet been drawn and the artificial lamps of reason lit. There was the deceptive conflict of the inward and the outward light. Not until the latter half of the century was a renewed and circumscribed security to be found whose foundation was the *cogito ergo sum* of Descartes.

The political storms which blew up over Europe at this time were not physically more horrible than those which had gone before, but they were more demoralizing. In the sixteenth century men had known very well what they were doing, whether they were poisoning rival princes in Italy, or harrying silver fleets in mid-Atlantic. It was a cocksure century. The seventeenth century was not. An anxious or resigned uncertainty, a doubt embracing both motives and aims obscured men's minds. Witchcraft and witch-hunting rose in horrible crescendo; astrology gained fantastic hold; extraordinary religions sprang up like mushrooms.

It is significant that only in the victorious, comfortable Dutch republic did a highly realist school of painting develop. Elsewhere the artist — with few exceptions — transmutes or subordinates reality. Even as sharp an observer as Callot handles his 'Misères de la Guerre' with a light and airy line. *Simplicissimus*, the nightmare novel of the Thirty Years War, was not written until a generation after the war itself, could not have been written until then. Compare the neat, topographical drawings done by Hollar when he accompanied Lord Arundel on an embassy to Germany at the height of the conflict, with the horrified jottings of Lord Arundel's secretary. The artist has deliberately closed his eyes. Compare also the symbolic grandeur of Rubens' painting of the Habsburg leaders meeting on the eve of the battle of Nördlingen: below, well-fed symbolic figures of the Danube and its tributaries, above the graceful young princely generals,

Spanish and Austrian, their cloaks and love-locks streaming in the wind, their left hands doffing, one the plumed sombrero, the other the Hungarian bonnet, their right hands clasped in brotherly greeting; behind each in artfully dissimilar groups the idealized officers of their staff; and beneath their clasped hands the distant spire of Nördlingen church. To-morrow will be fought the battle in which ten thousand men will die and the scattered remnants of a routed army carry disease and vermin from the Lech to the Rhine.

In civilizations, as in human beings, recognizable phenomena signalize certain epochs. In periods of transition an inward uneasiness is often expressed by affectations designed to conceal it; baroque performed this function in the civilization of Western Europe, bridging the gap between the crude assurance of the Renaissance and the polished assurance of the eighteenth century. All would ultimately yield again to man's control: science would be organized, the passions embanked, the arts regulated, religion reduced to formula; but in the meantime thoughts were directionless and men unhappy.

To this general oppression, a further weight was added in England. The young northern country of between three and four million inhabitants had recently come thrusting forward among the powers of Western Europe, had gained one or two spectacular successes against the gigantic power of Spain and suffered some ignominious checks. Her people, or rather her educated classes, accepted the former as the most natural thing in the world and blamed convenient scapegoats for the latter.

The phenomenal vigour and precosity of the Elizabethans had created a false expectation among their successors. The English knew already that they were the chosen people, their habitation a demi-paradise, their prowess by sea and land unmatched, their swords ever drawn and ever victorious in just causes. The deceits, the shifts, the betrayals, the total eclipse of the seventeenth century shook their faith in almost everything except their country. The

King, the Commons, the idle rich, the idle poor, the gentry, the City — you could take your choice which to blame, much as you can to-day. But nobody seems to have recognized the simple fact that England, with a quarter the population of France and a third that of Spain, with few discovered resources, with all her wealth in private hands, could not maintain the position she had inter-mittently reached under Elizabeth.

The total insignificance of their country in the European scene was all the harder for the average Englishman to understand, since it went with a period of comparative economic prosperity at home. One should not pay too much attention to the perennial English complaint that everything was going to the dogs, nor to evidence of local depressions. Local depressions there are always. Still less should one be misled by the poverty of the Crown; wealth was in private hands, and the Crown's powers of taxation were so limited that it had no means of tapping the wealth of the community either in its own or the public interest. But great wealth there certainly was, and the things which should — but do not always — go with wealth: a growing interest in the arts and education, leisure for thought and the cultivation of the graces.

Nor were wealth and civilization confined to the capital. England, a small country, was beginning to be fairly well roaded; communications improved, posts were instituted. If London con-tinued to be the only town of first-class importance, and the two universities the sources from which the intellectual life of London was fed, innumerable country houses were the centres of local constellations of talent. Everything points to a period of com-fort and ease such as the Elizabethans had hardly known.

All the more inexplicable, therefore, to contemporaries was the insignificance of their country in European politics. The indepen-dent gentry who stalwartly refused to give loans to the Crown were the first to throw up outraged hands when bankrupt pre-parations for war ended in disaster. 'Since England was England she got not so dishonourable a blow ...' The causes for which they cared were being betrayed and defeated on the continent of Europe, while their Government did nothing, or, fatally, too little. Puzzled, indignant, conscience-stricken, some of them volunteered in foreign armies. Others stayed at home and black-guarded their rulers. Still others justified the inglorious epoch, though for the wrong reasons:

> White Peace (the beautifull'st of things)
> Seems here her everlasting rest
> To fix, and spreads her downy Wings
>   Over the Nest:
>
> As when great Jove, usurping Reign,
> From the plagu'd World did her exile,
> And ty'd her with a golden Chain
>   To one blest Isle:
>
> Which in a Sea of plenty swam
> And turtles sang on every Bough,
> A safe retreat to all that came
>   As ours is now.

Thus Sir Richard Fanshawe, in 1630, a moment when religious liberty and the Protestant cause had been wiped out almost to the shores of the Baltic. Two years later, when the King of Sweden had smashed the Catholic armies back to the Danube and the younger generation in England strained at the leash to join in, another courtier, Thomas Carew, took up the refrain:

> ... What though the German drum
> Bellow for freedom and revenge, the noise
> Concerns not us, nor should divert our joys;
> Nor ought the thunder of their carabins
> Drown the sweet airs of our tun'd violins.

But it was not 'white Peace the beautifull'st of things' any more in the 1630s than in the 1930s; it was a wretched, uneasy peace with a bad conscience, and the tuned violins quivered with fore-boding.

Foreboding as much of inward as of outward disaster. The signs of political unrest in this country where the turtles were singing on every bough were apparent to anyone not blinded by its material prosperity. Church, State and society suffered from a succession of insignificant or unsuitable leaders. Intelligence was not lacking, but something — confidence, style, character even — was. The prestige of the Crown would hardly have survived any successor to Elizabeth; James I, who might have been a distinguished eccentric don, was clearly impossible. His son Charles acquired a tragic pathos at his latter end, but was not, reigning, an impressive king. The archbishops were little better: Bancroft portentous, not impressive, Abbot cantankerous and bigoted (having shot a beater while hunting, he was ultimately suspended for manslaughter: an unreassuring thing to happen to the archbishop), and last of all fussy little Laud, trotting briskly round snuffing out abuses. Society shook with the kind of scandals that had either been concealed, or been carried off with more style, in the days of Elizabeth: the Essex divorce, the Overbury murder trial, the case of Lord Audley, the prosecution of Lady Purbeck for adultery.

Small things, but educated England was a small, inbred society. This smallness gave importance to single personalities, and a negative importance to the lack of them.

A political crisis was evidently approaching at terrific speed. The government could not continue bankrupt in the 'sea of plenty'. Either the Crown must find means to tap the wealth of the country, or it must cede its authority to those who could. The same crisis had already broken in most European countries. Kings who could not be masters were liable to become victims. King James might survive; King Charles was obviously doomed. From Elizabeth's death in 1603 until 1630 the situation built up towards the crisis. Then came ten years of postponement when

Charles threw the opposition out of gear by refusing to call
Parliament. It was never anything but an unexpected interlude,
and never — except to those who were wilfully blind — appeared
as anything else. The inevitable clash was postponed for a decade,
the unrestful, mock-happy thirties.

> Ten years the world upon him falsely smiled
> Sheathing in fawning looks the deadly knife —

Fanshawe again, writing of the King his master; but he might be
speaking for many of his contemporary poets, for the whole of
his precocious generation.

The combination of spiritual unrest with material comfort —
a combination never again so strikingly apparent until our own
time — seems to be in England at least a fruitful one for poetry.
The astonishing harvest of the second quarter of the seventeenth
century has, reckoned in numbers alone, rarely been equalled.
But of this great population of poets very few made an attempt to
grapple with the problems of their times. The recurring note is, if
worldly, insouciance; if unworldly, retreat.

The two obvious exceptions, Milton and Marvell, were both to
be found among the opponents of the King. Milton is too complicated and individual a genius to conform to any general rules,
but in Marvell, born in 1621 and maturing as a poet during the
most restless and disastrous years of the century, many of the
characteristics of the Cavalier poets are apparent. He was un-
lucky by so narrow a margin in missing the interlude of the
thirties:

> The forward youth that would appear
> Must now forsake his Muses dear
> Nor in the shadows sing
> His numbers languishing.
>
> Tis time to leave the books in dust
> And oil the unuséd armour's rust ...

Unhappy 'forward youth', Marvell was only twenty-one when war broke out. The sense of threatened happiness was never more graphically expressed than in his

> But at my back I always hear
> Time's winged chariot hurrying near:
> And yonder all before us lie
> Deserts of vast eternity.

He, too, could retreat at times from the pressure of the world to embroider prettily on country themes. There are his glow-worms:

> Ye Country Comets, that portend
> No war, nor prince's funeral
> Shining unto no higher end
> Than to presage the grasses fall.
> Ye glow-worms, whose officious flame
> To wandering mowers shows the way ...

Evidently close kin to Herrick's glow-worms whose services were called in to light Julia to bed. Yet the bedrock of his poetry is not retreat, but acceptance and understanding. It is only necessary to compare the fearless political grasp displayed in his celebrated *Horatian Ode on Cromwell's Return from Ireland* with Abraham Cowley's *Ode to Charles I* after the first abortive Scots War. Marvell manages to compress a whole political theory as well as an extremely striking *aperçu* of the situation into his lines: Cowley makes no attempt to write anything but good verse. Neat and accomplished the empty phrases ring:

> Others by war their conquest gain
> You like a god your ends obtain
> Who when rude chaos for his help did call
> Spoke but the word and sweetly order'd all ...

The King had in fact been forced to yield to the Scots rebels without fighting because he realized in time that he had no army with which to fight them. Two years later, when he risked a war, the results were so disastrous that even Cowley had no words for them.

But the poets were mostly on the King's side. The reason can hardly have lain in the patronage afforded by the Court to literature. It was notoriously poor. The truth was that the poets of this period, however young and fashionable, belonged to the *arrière*, not to the *avant garde*. Their whole trend of thought reached back into a receding past, away from the cold and probing realism, both in thought and politics, which was gradually submerging the older world. They were in fact anti-political, just as the King's view was anti-political — an attempt to do without politics, not an attempt to reform them. This, in the political field the fatal weakness of the King's side, was its attraction for them, and its charm for posterity.

Revealed religion had dominated the dying world, and revealed religion is the refuge of one large group of these poets, the impregnable fortress into which they retreated from the anxious pressure of the time. Donne, from whom the poetic inspiration of his successors was partly derived, stands outside the group. He was thirty by the time Elizabeth died, and like all who reached manhood in that more robust epoch, his torments came mostly from within. There is no retreat in his religious verse, rather a fierce grappling with the mysteries of dogma and the hideous reality of death. He does not, like the later metaphysical poets, soar into the Empyrean, or abandon himself in feminine surrender to the arms of God. The earth is solid under him.

His successors, without exception, are in flight before the world; escape is their only message, whether they speak with the pellucid ingenuousness of Herbert, the lofty sweetness of Vaughan, the ecstasy of Crashaw, the liquid fluency of King, the vibrating rapture of Quarles. Occasionally and far off, one catches the echo of the world without:

> But hark! My pulse like a soft drum
> Beats my approach, tells thee I come,
> And slow howe'er my marches be,
> I shall at last sit down by thee.

The military simile has a hint of menace in King's peaceful elegy on his wife.

Each individual case is, of course, different. George Herbert, of noble birth, forsook the prospect of a worldly career for quiet at Bemerton; Henry Vaughan, a simple doctor in remote Brecknock, had little opportunity to know the world; Francis Quarles, who had been a courtier and travelled abroad, knew from what he was retreating; Henry King and Richard Crashaw felt the wind of politics at its keenest, the former losing his bishopric and, worse still, his library, the latter his Cambridge fellowship. King's quiet conscience and sweet disposition made his troubles the easier, and Crashaw, who died in poverty at Loretto, had found in the Catholic faith shelter from the blast.

Quarles, describing only his individual case, gives reason for them all:

> Like to the arctic needle, that doth guide
> The wand'ring shade by his magnetick pow'r,
> And leaves his silken Gnomon to decide
> The question of the controverted hour;
> First Franticks up and down, from side to side,
> And restless beats his crystall'd Iv'ry case
> With vain impatience: jets from place to place,
> And seeks the bosom of his frozen bride;
> At length he slacks his motion, and doth rest
> His trembling point at his bright Poles' beloved brest.

> Ev'n so my soul, being hurried here and there,
> By ev'ry object that presents delight,
> Fain would be settled, but she knows not where;
> She likes at morning what she loathes at night;

She bows to honour; then she lends an eare
To that sweet swan-like voice of dying pleasure,
Then tumbles in the scatter'd heaps of treasure;
Now flatter'd with false hope; now foyl'd with fear
Thus finding all the world's delights to be
But empty toyes, good God, she points alone to thee.

Less secure than this total retreat from the world was the mere
country retreat of Herrick, who lacked the quality of mind
necessary for more arduous contemplation than that of violets.
Not that he contemplated violets with much assiduity (he had at
first bitterly resented being cut off from the gaieties of the capital).
A close observation of nature is markedly absent from his, as from
most, contemporary verse. He evokes the colour and the climate
of the English summer with what proves to be on examination an
astonishing vagueness of accurate detail. Therein lies his genius.
Comfortably settled at Dean Prior in Devonshire, well connected,
by nature and breeding contentedly obsequious ('Great Caesar'
he apostrophizes the minuscule Charles I and wreathes verses like
garlands round the baby Duke of York), he was in a position to
bury his head, not in the sand, but in a bank of wild flowers. He
sang as he himself said

of Maypoles, hock-carts, wassails, wakes,
Of bridegrooms, brides and of their bridall cakes,
I write of Youth and Love and have Accesse
By them to sing of cleanly wantonnesse.

'Cleanly wantonnesse' — but for a few coarser outbursts at the
expense of personal enemies — does indeed hit off Herrick very
neatly. But his gifts, nourished on a diet of material, if simple,
pleasures could not apparently contend with adversity. Driven
out of his rectory, he was pleased at first with the prospect of
returning to London, but things were not what they had been, his
Great Caesar beheaded, his pretty Duke of York in exile, and well

on the way to becoming the far from pretty James II. The honey-suckle talent withered.

The fact was that in the seventeenth century — as in our own — escape was impossible. There is matter for reflection in the fact that its major poet, Milton, went out to meet the political problem of his time and to some extent subdued it to his verse. With few exceptions the others, when caught, were caught un-willingly. For there was no escape: not in contemplation at Little Gidding, not in the common rooms of Oxford and Cambridge, not in the rectories of Devonshire or the country mansions of the Cotswolds, least of all in the gardens of Whitehall. It was the politician's century, and the poet was already being pushed away, driven back, as it were, into his own society. Hence the flourish-ing of cliques, the Oxford clique with Will Cartwright, the Cambridge clique with Cowley and Crashaw, the 'sons' of Ben Jonson, the Whitehall clique of gentry. Hence the private jokes, the adulation of friends, the lampooning of enemies, the sly topical scandals and oblique references which make great tracts of their verse incomprehensible.

The false forward spring of the thirties brought on the flower-ing of innumerable talents; verses flowed gracefully from a hundred fluent quills, Carew, Davenant, Waller, Godolphin, Love-lace, Townshend, Habington. They were all quiet-needing talents, born in rich soil and germinated by showers of applause. Flower-ing in the sunshine of the thirties their delicate blossoms were later to fall unquickened or hang withered on the bough. But they were most of them, however short their bloom or few their verses, something more than mere fashionable practitioners of *vers d'occasion*. The anthological immortality of so many of the lyrics — an immortality which makes them too hackneyed for quotation — is itself a tribute to the astonishing felicity of their touch. 'Go lovely Rose', 'The lark now leaves his wat'ry nest', 'Tell me not, sweet, I am unkind' — each is unique, each perfect. Artificial in design, their poetry is yet unforced. Its effortlessness makes it at first glance seem almost too easy. There is nothing, not even observation, to give body to their works. Their natural phenomena are almost always wrong. Even gardens, a form of tamed and sophisticated nature in which they delighted, they never closely observed or accurately described. Yet at times their poetry seems all compact of sunlight and green lawns, of bright flowering borders and the white-thorn hedgerows of an English spring. Marvell's bees go to bed in the tulips, a freak of nature equalled by Lovelace's grasshopper snugly tucked up in a carved acorn. Their convention was not the laboured convention of accuracy. They relied on the rightness of sound and rhythm, and the associations which one happy phrase can call to mind. Their appeal is through the senses to the imagination, never laboriously to the inward eye which was Wordsworth's bliss of solitude but emphatically not theirs.

Imagination was their refuge, as faith was that of the metaphysical poets: imagination so strong that in most of them the poet and the man led separate lives. Some intrigued at Court, some planned a *coup d'état*, some when war came raised troops of horse, many distinguished themselves in the field and more in the dangerous parts of spies and messengers. Their experience of life was vivid, harsh and dangerous, anxious and despairing, the experience of the defeated. Hardly a breath of it reaches their verse, unless it be a soft melancholy like that of a summer evening: life is short, beauty is shorter, and the cool shadow of not unwelcome death lengthens across the garden.

The *carpe diem* theme recurs in innumerable variations. Lighthearted in Cowley's

> To-day is ours, what do we fear?
> To-day is ours, we have it here.
> Let's treat it kindly that it may
> Wish at least with us to stay.

Didactic in Herrick's 'Gather ye Rosebuds,' *moqueur* in Jordan's

irrefutable statement that his mistress 'will be damnable mouldy
a hundred years hence', faintly menacing in Jasper Mayne's

> Time is the feather'd thing
> And, whilst I praise
> The sparklings of thy looks and call them rays
> Takes wing.
> Leaving behind him as he flies
> An unperceivéd dimness in thine eyes.

But apart from this general preoccupation with the shortness of
time, they search after beauty rather than truth, manner and not
matter. Occasionally, but very occasionally, genuine personal
feeling forces a way through. Cowley's lament for his friend
William Harvey opens on a note almost harsh with pain:

> It was a dismal and a fearful night,
> Scarce could the Morn drive on th' unwilling light,
> When sleep death's image left my troubled breast
> By something liker death possessed,
> My eyes with tears did uncommanded flow
> And on my soul hung the dull weight
> Of some intolerable fate.
> What bell was that? Ah me! Too much I know.

But this is the exception. For death, however keenly felt, as for
love, however genuine, there were the accepted patterns, the
tender, plaintive strain, the Grecian vegetation, the mourning
shepherds. Life could be met only on these terms, feeling
expressed only under the customary disguises. From the country
peace of Bemerton George Herbert mildly protested:

> Is it no verse, except enchanted groves
> And sudden arbours shadow coarse-spunne lines?
> Must purling streams refresh a lover's loves?
> Must all be vail'd, while he that reads, divines,
> Catching the sense at two removes?

George Herbert could dispense with such veils. The 'sweet and vertuous soul' had made peace with heaven and had no more to fear on earth. He was lucky, too, in dying before the crisis of the time.

But for those who must go on living in the world the pretence was essential. Unlike Milton, they were not on terms with it. So while the King's government went finally bankrupt, while the Scots overran the northern counties, while Strafford was beheaded in front of a gigantic crowd of jubilant spectators, and the little Archbishop escaped by a back way from the mob and the King fled the capital and the Queen fled the country, and after a hundred and fifty years of peace England was at war with herself, these poets were imploring Amarantha to unravel her hair, giving the nightingale winter quarters in their lady's throat, asserting that birds and flowers mistook her coming for the dawn, with a hundred other irrelevancies.

When the assumed mood breaks down, it gives place to a venomous or ribald parody on itself. Equivocal words and a whole alphabet of symbols invest the pretty gallantries with other meanings. Most of these poets are adept at disguising obscenity; Suckling's sleight of hand is positively insolent. From his brilliantly accomplished verse, indeed, a savage, go-getting, to-morrow-we-die materialism emerges almost naked. Gambler and society playboy, he never had any doubt of the fate in store for the lilies of the field, planned to have his good time and had it. Whether or not he killed himself, preferring poison to an uglier end, is a matter of indifference; but he died in Paris and in poverty during the opening months of the Civil War. The first whiff of gunpowder had been enough for him.

His fellows, more sympathetic for that reason, cultivated their wilful blindness to the end, their 'careless heads with roses bound' within the doomed walls of Basing House or besieged Oxford, in the shadow of the firing party and the block. Montrose, like Raleigh, was rhyming on the eve of execution. Nor did they mean, as one literal-minded editor has thought, that roses were commonly twined in their hair. The roses were their still lovely imaginings, though the draught whistled under the door in the fireless prison, and a querulous wife with a sheaf of unpayable bills was the material out of which they conjured Althea 'whispering at the grates'.

Theirs was a mental, not a physical, shrinking. Few of them actually failed in courage. Suckling, not unexpectedly, Waller, too; sensitive and vain, with most of his relations on the Parliament side, he fancied himself as an orator in the House of Commons. Later, becoming involved in a plot to betray London to the King, he lost his nerve and betrayed his associates instead, an act which forty subsequent years of blameless life could not altogether wipe out.

> The soul's dark cottage batter'd and decay'd
> Lets in new light through chinks that time hath made,

he was to write long after, in a poem whose twelve lines sum up perhaps more perfectly than anything else in the English language the mistakes of youth and the regrets of age. None can have known them better.

But Davenant was knighted for valour by the King and employed on dangerous missions. Falling into Parliamentary hands, he was only saved from execution, as some thought, by the intervention of Milton. Cowley, expelled like Crashaw from Cambridge, entered the Queen's service as a secretary and was employed as a confidential agent during the Commonwealth. It did his talent no good. He was never to fulfil the promise of his radiant teens. Sidney Godolphin was killed in a skirmish at Chagford; Cartwright died of camp fever in overcrowded Oxford; Denham, Cleveland, Lovelace, Fanshawe, all were active for the King, and all were dispossessed, imprisoned or exiled.

In debts, defeat and hunger their voices fade out. A few

naturally carried over the tradition, with the remains of their lives, into the ensuing period. The individual always exists to blur the lines which historians for convenience must draw precisely. Traherne, born late in the 1630s, closes the exquisite cycle which began with Quarles. The Restoration brought with it the triumph of the scientific approach, the foundation of the Royal Society, and the cynical shelving of moral values which accompanied the new outlook. Smooth, ingenious and satirical was the new and more ordered expression of the poetic impulse. Fantasy and faith were alike dead: they had been the last expression of the nation's wondering and ingenuous adolescence, of a time when men still saw themselves midway between the beasts and the angels. Henceforward man was lord of creation: there was nothing he would not know. The limitless world, inexplicable and impressive, dwindled to the compass of his mind. Descartes, Boyle, Newton – the physical and mental map regained its contours. Men knew once more where they were and whither they were going, but their fancy would never again range so freely, and no one again would say

> I saw Eternity the other night
> Like a great ring of pure and endless light.

THE STRATEGY OF THE GREAT CIVIL WAR[1]

THE Civil Wars of England lasted, with one long intermission, for about nine years. It was in September 1642 that first blood was drawn in a skirmish at the village of Powick Bridge opposite Worcester on the Tème, and in September again, nine years later, that the battle of Worcester ended the war, almost in the same fields. The spatter of scars from musket balls on the south wall of Powick church tower is from the later, not the earlier, battle.

The political significance of the Civil Wars is so great that their military history has been, if not positively neglected, at least submerged. Not entirely, of course, for Cromwell's organization of the New Model Army and Rupert's famous cavalry have been obvious subjects of study. But Clarendon, the leading historian of the war, was a civilian, and few of those who fought, certainly neither of its two outstanding soldiers, were great hands with the pen. Cromwell's dispatches are brief, tough, impressive, but throw all too little light on the purely military side of the war. Rupert, a proud and silent man, neither boasted of his victories nor explained his defeats. 'It is a life of honour,' he said of a soldier's career, 'but a dog would not lead it.'

The Civil War is part of our political heritage; the principles for which our ancestors fought are still alive to us. It is part of the literary and romantic tradition of this country, bringing back nostalgic visions of fluttering banners and Van Dyck faces, of vain heroism and thundering cavalry charges, of stern-faced men with Bible and sword going into battle to the chanting of a psalm. For most of us it is a part of our childhood, for who has not played Cavaliers and Roundheads? But we do not easily fit these

[1] *The Geographical Magazine.*

imaginative pictures to what we know of the English countryside, and the battle-fields of the Great Civil War remain for the most part neglected sites. Occasionally there will be a monument to some distinguished casualty — Hampden has an obelisk at Chalgrove Field; Falkland, Sunderland and Carnarvon share another at Newbury; but at Naseby the monument is in the wrong place and at Edgehill it is the wrong monument, for the grey monolith on the side of the steep slope where the trees end was erected to a soldier who fought at Waterloo.

The strategy of the Civil War in its larger aspects has not been much studied, and this is understandable for the English Civil War is a curiosity of military history with rules of its own outside the ordinary line of development. Its strategy was bound up, one might almost say swaddled up, with the social structure of the country and limited by the peculiarities of the political situation; it could not be planned according to the military rules and practice of continental fighting, but was amenable to the brilliant manipulation of talented amateurs. It was indeed a war in which the professional soldier was at a disadvantage. Of the numerous Englishmen who had been trailing their pikes in Flanders for want of employment at home and who hurried back to fight either for King or Parliament, few achieved any real distinction, though many were efficient and experienced in the minutiae of their profession. Thomas Fairfax, a man whose sheer thoroughness and determination (he was a Yorkshireman) amounted nearly to genius, and the brilliant, unstable George Goring were perhaps the only two professional soldiers who made any significant mark. More often professional ideas interfered with the freedom of invention and action which English conditions offered.

It is significant that the two men who best understood and exploited the situation were both, if not exactly amateurs, at least beginners in their profession. Cromwell knew nothing whatever of warfare before he acquired his captain's commission in the summer of 1642, and Rupert, although he had served in the Netherlands and Germany, as a ranker in the Prince of Orange's life-guard and later as an officer, had spent his last four years as a prisoner of war when, at the age of twenty-two, he was appointed Lieutenant-General of the King's Cavalry. Cromwell was therefore too ignorant and Rupert too young to be bound by the accepted rules.

The civilian population, too, was ignorant of the rules. No war had been fought in England for a century and a half and the attitude of a fat and prosperous people, used to orderly government, was very different from the embittered, helpless resignation of the German and Flemish peasantry. Foreign towns knew only too well the blackmail of *Brandschatzung* — the indemnity which the General of an occupying army demanded in return for preventing the sack of the town. English towns had never heard of such a thing, and when Rupert, assuming the existence of the custom, exacted a sum from Leicester, great was the indignation of the city fathers and great the speed with which King Charles ordered his nephew to pay it back. It was the first rule of continental warfare which had to be unlearnt in England, for here each side strove not to terrorize, but to pacify and win over the civil population.

Whence, among this peaceful people, arose the armies which appeared with such terrifying speed in the summer of 1642? England had an antiquated system of defence, the local levies. These hastily mustered yokels were almost entirely untrained, and although provision was supposed to be made for their equipment, very little was ever to be had; a few old pikes with a helmet or two of an Elizabethan model were often as much as could be found for them.

London had its trained bands who had been exercised occasionally in the handling of pikes on fine summer evenings. The King, fearing trouble with the people, had created a small life-guard shortly before the outbreak of the war. For the rest both sides relied on troops of volunteers raised by wealthy or patriotic gentlemen who defrayed the expenses themselves, recruiting the men on their own estates and arming them according to their own caprice. If they chose to equip them with battle-axes or bows and arrows — and on occasion we find both of these anti-quated weapons in use — to tie coloured ribbons on their shoulders or encase them from top to toe in armour — as did Sir Arthur Hazelrig with a regiment immediately nicknamed the 'Lobsters' — no one was going to stop them.

The armies of both sides, therefore, presented a variegated appearance. Some were too much armed, some were not armed at all; there was uniformity neither of equipment nor dress. Some wore red, some wore blue, some undyed cloth — they would dye it in the blood of their enemies. No definite mark distinguished the King's men from Parliament's. Officers of the Royalist forces wore red sashes, Parliamentary officers orange, but it is not to be supposed that the supply of sashes was at first equal to the sudden demand, nor that the reds and oranges hastily bought up or fished out of the oak chest by a thrifty wife did not vary through every shade and approximate inconveniently to each other. Mistakes between friend and foe were frequent and often bloody. A further confusion was added during the opening phase of the war by the Parliamentarian habit of referring to the Royalists as the 'rebels' and themselves as the party of King and Parliament. (One remembers Hampden's device: Not against the King I fight, but for the King and the Commons' right.) Some enthusiastic French gentlemen who had hurried over to England to defend their countrywoman, Queen Henrietta Maria, enlisted in error under the wrong flag.

As well as the victims of such strange misunderstandings there was a fluctuating fringe of professional soldiers who changed sides to suit themselves; some were Scots or Irish mercenaries, some Englishmen, one or two came from farther afield, like that Croatian Captain of whom John Aubrey tells, who openly

declared: 'I care not for your cause but for your half-crowns and
your handsome women.'

To the professional trained abroad there was no dishonour in
changing sides. The arrangement was a business contract, and an
officer who resigned his commission in one continental army
was wholly at liberty to take up a commission in another when
he wished. Whole regiments shifted from side to side during the
Thirty Years War with no one thinking the worse of them. But
in this matter the English war proved to be different. We hear
significantly much of prisoners. There was a concentration camp
for Royalist soldiers at Coventry, and atrocity stories were told
of the sufferings of Parliamentarians in Oxford Castle and of the
King's men lodged in the hulks of moored vessels in the Thames.
As for the Royalist officers, the Tower of London had rarely
been more fully or more gaily populated.

> When flowing cups run swiftly round
> With no allaying Thames,
> Our careless heads with roses bound
> Our hearts with loyal flames . . .

The question of prisoners was one on which the rulings of
the foreign-trained professionals were an inadequate guide: in the
German wars large numbers of prisoners were not taken; the
defeated were simply absorbed into the army of the victor. But
the English quaintly regarded changing sides as dishonourable;
it might be done but never with credit. 'Walter Baskervile',
we read in the contemptuous jottings of a Royalist soldier, 'first
for the Parliament, then for the King, then theirs, then taken
prisoner by us, and with much adoe gott his pardon and now
pro rege, God wott.'

In other ways, too, the spirit of the English forces was peculiar
to these islands. The rank and file, recruited from the peasantry
from Wales, Cornwall, West Yorkshire, Lancashire and Cheshire
on the King's side, from the eastern and the home counties on

Parliament's, shared a strong spirit of individualism and independence. We speak loosely of the survival of 'feudalism' in England, thinking of our ancient landed gentry and the sentiments of loyalty and obligation between squire and tenantry; but in fact feudalism in its final form never developed in England, and the last vestiges of anything which a man from the Continent would have called feudal had vanished a century before the Civil War. No English landowner had rights of life and death over his people; few, if any, English peasants were rigidly bound to the soil. The troops which followed the standards of their local gentry were, taken by and large, more humane, more civilized, more reasonable than their counterparts abroad. But they were also more stubborn, more argumentative and, until they had commanders who understood them, less trainable. Added to this, some of them took a stand on their rights and could not be gainsaid.

The men of the local levies refused to fight outside their own counties, which was indeed one of the presumed conditions of their service, and it was only with extraordinary persuasion that Sir Ralph Hopton managed to bring the Cornish infantry — the finest in the Royalist army — out of its native duchy, nor in spite of a plan of campaign which was intended to end only in the recapture of London, did this particular section of the King's army ever appear farther east than Devizes, where at Roundway Down they had the pleasure of tumbling Sir Arthur Hazelrig's ridiculously encased 'Lobsters' down one of the steepest chalk slopes in the Wiltshire downs.

A further problem in discipline and organization was set by the gentlemen volunteers, who, although only a sprinkling of the whole army and usually grouped together into a troop, were a perennial obstruction to discipline. The gentry of England knew nothing of war — again how un-feudal! — and carried both their pleasant manners, their social distinctions and their strong individuality into battle. At that time nobody was brought up on the military doctrine of 'theirs not to make reply, theirs not to reason why'. They answered back and reasoned why in and out of season, with the utmost nonchalance. What a world of obstructive young subalterns is conjured up by the ingenuous tribute paid by Waller to Cromwell, who, as a junior officer, 'did not argue upon his orders'.

After more than a century of peace England was naturally behind Europe in her armaments, a fact which for once did not matter, since no foreign nation was involved. The demand for arms in the opening months of the war far outran the supply, and officers coming back from abroad must have laughed to see the antiquated pikes and Elizabethan helmets in the ranks of both armies. Everything was in short supply. Birmingham manufacturers, cashing in on the King's necessity, put out a line in cheap swords, for a consignment of which Charles contracted, until Prince Rupert, raging over hundreds of snapped weapons, threatened to resign if his cavalry were issued with any more 'Brummagem Blades'. English pistols too seem at first to have been oddly unreliable: they would go off suddenly, backwards, or misfire altogether. Or perhaps they were only mishandled by amateur soldiers. Prince Rupert, a singularly striking target and frequently the object of deliberate attentions, got through the whole war with nothing but a graze on the shoulder, which suggests a low standard of aiming. It was poor Sir George Lisle, facing the firing squad after the surrender of Colchester, who called to his executioners to come closer, and when they would not, pleaded: 'Friends, I have been nearer when you have missed me.'

Heavy artillery played a larger part than has generally been allowed. It was of inestimable value in sieges, and the Civil War was a great war of sieges. Transport was a perennial problem, for the cannon were enormously heavy for their power, would stick in the muddy roads holding up the progress of an entire army, and as often as not leave a wheel behind them when forcibly hauled out. Yet, in spite of the difficulty of transport, guns were used conventionally in the continental manner in pitched battle, where they pounded away to very little effect before the opening of the action. When Cromwell in 1648 left his entire artillery behind while he raced in advance to cut off the Scots Royalists at Preston, he was sacrificing superiority in armaments to speed and surprise in a way which a conventional soldier of the time would have thought absurdly dangerous. His decision was fully justified by the event.

But in siege warfare the cannon was really important, and indeed the King's weakness in this arm was certainly one of the factors in his defeat. The battering power of the big culverins and demi-culverins, twenty-pounders and twelve-pounders respectively at close range—about 300 yards—was terrific. A sustained bombardment would smash down the average city wall effectively enough for the besiegers to fight their way in, and comparatively few cities failed to surrender after a serious bombardment.

Banbury was an outstanding exception, for here the Royalist colonel, Sir William Compton, a boy of nineteen, kept the garrison working in shifts day and night throwing up an earthwork behind the outer wall until, after fourteen weeks' resistance, he was at length relieved. Colchester, in 1647, surrendered not so much to hunger as to superior artillery. The batteries of the defenders gave out for lack of ammunition and Fairfax was able to move his heavy guns into a position from which they could have raked the town. Gloucester, besieged by the King in 1643, held out until the trained bands of London, in a fervour of devotion, marched across the Cotswolds to its rescue, simply because the King had not enough ammunition for his guns, and so could not smash his way in. The capture of Waller's guns at the otherwise small skirmish of Cropredy Bridge turned it into an event of importance to the King, and it is notable that at the second battle of Newbury Prince Maurice carried out an elaborate and dangerous manœuvre in order to secure the King's artillery, first collecting the guns into Donnington Castle and posting a guard over them, then retiring to Oxford, collecting reinforcements and making a lightning advance across the Berkshire downs by night to Donnington, to convoy the guns safely back into Oxford. Not for nothing did the Parliamentarians call Maurice, Rupert's less spectacular brother, the 'good come-off'.

The musket was the most important fire-arm in general use in the seventeenth century, and the musketeers were a class apart, the aristocrats of the infantry. In England, a country even in those days of ditches and copses, and deep lanes fringed with hedges, a skilful captain could do wonders with a handful of musketeers. We find them lining the long hedge on the Royalist right flank at Naseby field, preventing Fairfax from manœuvring his army or outflanking the King. We find them contesting the transverse hedges and orchard walls in the first battle of Newbury, an engagement which was not so much a pitched battle as a cross-word puzzle of single skirmishes in the enclosed market gardens and orchards on the outskirts of the little town. When during the battle Falkland, the King's Secretary of State, tired of a conflict to which he saw no profitable end, rode his horse at a gap in one of the hedges, he knew that there would be musketeers on either side to pick him off; and accordingly found the death he sought. At Langport, where George Goring made the last serious stand for the King against the triumphant Parliamentarian advance into the west in 1645, he held the ridge above the town by investing the narrow lane, which was its only access, with the main strength of his musketeers. A narrow English lane, covered by musketry fire, was a death trap to incautious cavalry. But Fairfax threw in the whole strength of his infantry to fight the Royalists back, foot by foot, at push of pike, from the knotted thorn trees and the high banks.

In hand-to-hand contest it was push of pike which ultimately decided the issue. And the pike, for all its simplicity, was an effective weapon when skilfully handled, both in attack and defence. The continental pikemen could withstand or at least break the impetus of cavalry attack; the attitude of defence was a lunge, the butt end of the pike resting against the instep of the hinder foot, the shaft steadied against the bent forward leg. In this attitude the skilful pikeman could fend off attack with the point of the pike controlled by the left hand, and keep his right hand free for sword play.

Could the London trained bands have done anything so complicated? Doubt seems permissible. As for the country levies, they found other uses for their pikes — when they had them. They were convenient for flicking the fruit off orchard trees, for hooking a new shirt from the housewife's line: they could be turned to account for hanging up a cooking-pot, punting a ferry across a stream, or even for chopping wood. 'I cannot conceive what these fellows are doing with their weapons', grumbled Sir Ralph Hopton when yet another batch of infantrymen reported irrecoverable damage or loss.

The general strategy of the Civil War is obscured by innumerable local quarrels. Parliament strove from the outset to coordinate its supporters into associations and groups, of which the most important was the Eastern Association from which sprang Cromwell's army and the ultimate reorganization of the New Model. The King, paradoxically, diffused his energies and played up to local magnates in order to gain widespread support and undermine his opponents throughout the country. In pursuit of this system he fatally dispersed his forces. By garrisoning isolated country houses he reduced the effective strength of the army which he was able to put in the field, and in the end the Royalist war came to a close in a series of heroic and useless resistances before, one after another, the fortified manors and fair country seats hauled down the royal standard. Some, like Basing House, fell only to assault and paid the penalty in the blood of the defenders.

One peculiarity of the English landscape assisted time and again in the reduction of these improvised fortresses. This was the position of the village church, so often within a stone's throw of the manor. With its strong square tower the typical village church made a convenient station for a gun, by the threat of which the neighbouring house could be driven to surrender.

Before the King's main army was broken at Naseby and the isolated garrisons successively reduced, many had been the local fights and skirmishes between the small forces in these outposts and Parliamentary troops passing through the country. In the same way, though not so frequently, nests of Parliamentarians recruited and held together by local magnates molested passing Royalists, and in some stretches of country which saw none of the serious fighting, local jealousies and local quarrels kept up spasmodic disturbance.

The main strategic outline of the war is, nevertheless, plain enough. The chief strength of Parliament lay in the south and east; of the King in the north and west. He unfurled his standard in Nottingham, the most southerly point at which he could cross the Trent, in August 1642, struck south across the Midlands collecting his forces, intending to march at once to London. The Parliamentary army under Essex barred his way below the sharp ridge of Edgehill in Warwickshire, but was sufficiently damaged in the action which followed on October 23rd to make the capitulation of the city something more than a possibility. But Charles hesitated fatally and by the time his advance guard reached Turnham Green — the main strength of his army carrying Brentford by assault — the trained bands had come to stop him and London was in a state of defence, with chains and barricades across the city streets and the Bowling Green at Hyde Park Corner the pivotal point of a system of outer defences of earthworks and batteries.

The King, however, decided to fall back no farther than Oxford, thus making his headquarters at the apex of a triangle, of which the bases were in Lancashire, Wales and the South-West, extending forward into enemy territory. The Chilterns, with their steep north-westward face against the King, were to prove an insuperable barrier to any bold frontal attack on London; the town of Reading, in the only practicable gap, was bitterly contested, changing hands four times in the course of the war. The strategy planned by Prince Rupert for the reduction of London during the following year, 1643, was the separate advance of the King's forces from the north and west in a pincer movement which was to converge on the estuary of the Thames just below the capital. He did not believe that this port and merchant city would hold out in the face of a threat to its very life-blood, the sea-ward approaches. He was probably right, but the plan came to nothing owing to the difficulty of moving the armies so far from their recruiting grounds. The men of the western midlands would not advance on London while the Parliamentary stronghold of Gloucester remained unreduced in their rear. The west country men feared with equal reason the raiding of their homes and fields by the Parliamentary garrison which still held Plymouth, and the town of Kingston-upon-Hull was a menace to Yorkshire. The King's two fatal weaknesses prevented him from reducing these three cities. He failed at Gloucester for lack of artillery, and at Plymouth and Hull because such navy as there was had declared for Parliament and kept the garrisons revictualled from the sea.

In the following year, Rupert attempted to save the situation by a double preliminary campaign for the reduction of all subsidiary Parliamentary forces in the west and north before the march on London. The western campaign succeeded with the surrounding and surrender of the Earl of Essex, but the northern campaign ended in disaster at Marston Moor on July 3rd, 1644. It was a pitched battle which Rupert had not intended to fight, and which was forced on him because Charles's military advisers in Oxford feared that the city might be attacked if the absence of the army were prolonged. In the circumstances one cannot but feel that the choice of so exposed and indefensible a site as Oxford for his headquarters was a disastrous handicap to the King.

The loss of the north was fatal to Charles's hopes. Moreover, the Parliamentary army had now been reorganized under Fairfax and Cromwell. The strength of the Royalist army was annihilated at Naseby in June 1645 and the final mopping-up of the King's scattered garrisons was merely a matter of time and patience. Attempts on the part of the King to stabilize a front farther to the west along the line of the Severn and behind the Cotswolds, with his headquarters at Worcester, failed completely. His last army, from the midlands and Wales, was surrounded and capitulated at Stow-on-the-Wold in March 1646, his last western army at Truro a week earlier.

Parliamentary strategy, for the first part of the war, being purely defensive, was less interesting. It was also uninspired. In fact the Parliamentary side produced no strategist of the stature of Rupert. What it had was a superb tactician in Cromwell. Cromwell realized that until Parliament had cavalry which could out-manœuvre Rupert's they would never be able to pass from defence to attack, and he set himself to develop that cavalry methodically, with infinite patience, making of his heavy-armed, perfectly disciplined, but swift and mobile Ironsides the model for the cavalry of the New Model Army.

Indeed, when we think of that war, of the English countryside alive with the troops of the seventeenth century, it is always of the cavalry that we think. For the whole conformation of the land cried out for the exploitation of this arm. The wide stretches of unfenced common land, the huge sweep of the Wiltshire and Berkshire downs, the innumerable dents and hollows, rises and depressions of the midlands, made it the perfect country for cavalry fighting – not for pitched battles between charging squadrons of horse, although that might come in, but for skirmishing and raiding. It was the sort of country in which a small number of cavalry, cleverly used, might baffle, divide and defeat far larger forces. Which was precisely what Rupert, left to himself, was perpetually trying to do; as when dodging with lightning speed across the Yorkshire dales he drew the besiegers off from York and slipped in to the relief of the city from the north, while Fairfax was still looking about for him on the western side.

Moreover, cavalry had another advantage for these ill-provided armies, since horse and man could themselves be used as a weapon. Continental cavalry was armed largely with pistols and until the time of Gustavus Adolphus the 'caracole' had been the favourite tactic; each line of cavalry halted, fired, and having fired wheeled off to the rear to wait for their next turn. There was no actual contact with the opposing force. Gustavus preferred the terrifying method of charging without a halt straight into the ranks opposite, firing only at the last minute. Rupert, whose troops, as we have seen, were poorly armed, taught his men to rely almost entirely on shock and impact. He turned horse and man into projectiles, and both at Edgehill and Naseby simply rode down the opposing ranks until they panicked and fled. Cromwell copied and developed the method, improving the armour and equipment of his troops, until the impact of the Ironsides became like the impact of so many miniature tanks. Sheer weight drove them through the enemy.

Just as the English open country was specially suited to the swift and free movement of small bodies of cavalry, so the hedged lanes, the ditches and the banks gave special opportunities to the musketeers. In contrast to the wide scope of cavalry action were the many congested engagements fought out between infantry in the built-up and enclosed outskirts of many a quiet English town, or even in the outbuildings of some large manor-house. When the owners of Compton Wynyates attempted to recapture their house, fortified against them by the Parliamentarians, the outer wall of the park, the inner garden wall, the stable yards became successive points of a frantic and embittered defence. In few wars can there have been quite so many actions in narrowly enclosed spaces or improvised strong-points. The country had few fortresses in a condition of readiness, so fortresses must be made as occasion demanded and offered. In one church at least, Alton in Hampshire, a band of trapped Royalists defended the length of the nave pier by pier, barricading themselves behind pews and tables, surrendering at last on the chancel steps. The conversion of Lichfield Cathedral into a fortress was a more deliberate act, for the Cathedral dominates the town; twice defended it was twice taken, and a great part of its fine red-sandstone Gothic destroyed in the process.

The English climate has not altered very much in three hundred years. Naseby was fought 'about the noon of a glorious day in June', but Naseby was exceptional. The summers of the Civil War were typical summers; 'a blustring cold day, and the evening very wett', or some equally depressing entry, is found time and again in the notes of the contemporaries. That particular blustering cold day was in August. One can sympathize too with the Musketeers who were to 'go resolutely forth by Sallies, in a dark, cold, blustring, rainy, tempestuous night'. We all know such nights. But the climate was not subject to great extremes and therefore we hear less than we do in continental fighting of the formal business of going into winter quarters and abandoning further manœuvres until the spring. If the larger movements of the war were, as one would expect, seasonal, there was intermittent fighting all the year round. Ice was on the ground in some parts of England in the August of 1642, but the winters themselves were for the most part mild and muggy.

The Civil War was the last prolonged or serious war to be fought in England itself, and centuries of peace have wiped away the scars. Here and there an ancient helmet or a pair of rusty spurs hang in a local museum; here and there a church wall is scarred with small shot, an ancient font carries the scratched initials of the soldiers who camped there, or a country house will preserve by oral tradition the story of some private act of heroism, like the story of Arthur Jones's wife and her cool deluding of the Parliamentary soldiers to save her husband's life, which is handed down at Chastleton.

It is hard to see Turnham Green or even Newbury as once they were, and Wigan is no longer the 'pretty village' through which Prince Rupert rode after his relief of Latham House; yet you may trace Cromwell's position with tolerable certainty on the rolling fields of Naseby and follow his brilliant manœuvres on the bald expanse of Marston Moor, or, walking the by-roads of England, see suddenly that trivial hillock, this unimportant brook re-endowed with the terrible significance of some brief and bloody afternoon three hundred years ago.

THE GERMAN MYTH[1]

ALL normal human beings are interested in their past. Only when the interest becomes an obsession, overshadowing present action and future conduct, is it a danger. In much the same way healthy nations are interested in their history, but a morbid preoccupation with past glories is a sign that something is wrong with the constitution of the State. It is found among scattered and broken peoples, among the declining and impoverished, among the parvenu or recently restored. I am not here speaking of a merely learned preoccupation with the past, but rather of that romantic concern with ancient splendours which is expressed by the resuscitation of forgotten and long out-dated customs, the injudicious reproduction of ancient architectural styles, the creation of unnecessary monuments, and the prostitution of historiography to modern 'patriotic' purposes.

Most nations have passed through periods of this kind. History, in spite of the occasional protest of historians, will always be used in a general way as a collection of political and moral precedents. But there is a distinction in the methods by which it is so used, a distinction between argument and statement. There is an important difference between the deduction of a principle from certain given facts, and the emotional prejudice which endows the facts themselves with preternatural significance. Few nations can safely cast stones in this matter. But in no European country has the tendency been so marked as in Germany. The preoccupation of the German people with their past, their bewildered reverence for it, their clumsy and repeated attempts to endow their confused political story with symbolic meaning, are symptoms of profound national ill-health.

The traveller in Germany sees on every side evidence of a

[1] *The Tablet*, April 25th, 1942.

romantic-symbolic 'let's pretend' attitude to national history. This misunderstanding of the past is combined with a sometimes crafty, sometimes ingenuous, attempt to blend it with the present. German history lacks outward unity. All the greater, therefore, is the desire to endow it with mystic oneness. Hence the emphasis on *Einheit* — unity — in German patriotic literature and in German text-books. The most improbable places have been found for blazoning this lesson: as for instance on the sword-blade of the gigantic statue of Arminius, erected on the dubious site of his victory over the Roman legions in the Teutoburgerwald. The figure of the ancient Teutonic chief, 186 feet high from the base of the arched substructure to the tip of the upraised sword, dominates the landscape and brandishes in the face of heaven the inscribed legend:

> Germany's unity, my strength,
> My strength, Germany's strength.

The conception is a nineteenth-century one, as indeed is the whole Arminius legend in its present form.

He is a strange figure, this Arminius, typical of the confused thinking which has gone on round German history. One of the many quarrelsome barbarian chieftains in the partially conquered lands beyond the Rhine, he had the intelligence to realize that he could only make a stand against the Romans by persuading his fellows to enter into alliance with him. He had also the necessary force of character and military skill to hold the ephemeral alliance together long enough to bring the Romans to decisive battle. The achievement was a considerable one, though not as stupendous as the German legend has made it. This grand old Germanic figure unhappily perished in the grand old Germanic way: not long after his victory he was murdered by other jealous chieftains. The main source for the story of Arminius is in Tacitus. It was here that Ulrich von Hutten found it early in the sixteenth century; he was the first German propagandist to see its possibilities, but he saw them through the eyes of a sixteenth-century anti-clerical as much as of an early German nationalist — indeed at that time the two were closely knit. Arminius represented to him the native *secular* force of Germany. Not until very much later does the Arminius legend again creep into the political field, this time with a purely nationalist bearing. With the revival of the German language and the revolt against foreign fashions in the later eighteenth century, enterprising publicists were bound to exploit Arminius yet again. One writer in a macabre fantasy called *Besuch um Mitternacht* conjured up the pure-bred barbarian chief to reproach a German prince impatiently waiting for his Italian mistress.

Nevertheless, Arminius missed fire as a popular figure. He was too uncouth perhaps, too remote from the complicated, stuffy world of the eighteenth and nineteenth centuries. Kleist's play about him, for instance, although written in 1808, was not printed before the author's death, and did not reach the stage until after the Franco-Prussian War. It has held it more or less ever since, but one suspects a dutiful rather than a spontaneous response from the generality of the public. Arminius in fact continues to be a text-book, rather than a genuinely popular, national hero, although where he does touch an occasional faithful heart, he certainly evokes an extravagant devotion. The sculptor who designed his monument spent nearly forty years on this labour of love, and died within a few months of its unveiling: life had no more to offer.

A yet more confusing example of German historical mythification is presented in the well-known Barbarossa legend. This is a real piece of folk-lore, ancient and very widespread, long before Rückert's poem and the nineteenth-century imperial revival gave it its text-book currency. There seems to be all over Europe, and for all I know beyond it as well, a kind of necessity for national heroes to retain a dim, sleeping immortality in the secret places of the mountains, ready to return when their time shall come. Several mountains in Germany — one of which is significantly near to Berchtesgaden — dispute the honour of being the resting place of Barbarossa. Traced to its foundations, however, this legend, too, shows a tendency to resolve itself into meaningless fragments. In the first place, the original legend had nothing to do with the immensely solid, foursquare, unspiritual figure of Barbarossa. It was whispered first of his grandson, Frederick II, that extraordinary man with his incomprehensible scientific interests, and his oriental morals, who caught the popular fancy of Western Europe by his recapture of Jerusalem. It mattered little to the Germans that he had spent only a small part of his reign among them, and done nothing whatever for their development as a nation. Nobody at that time cared very deeply about nations as such. The struggle was between Papacy and Empire, between the claims of the spiritual and the universal, and the material and particularist; it reached its dramatic height under the leadership of this brilliant, ruthless giant. To half Europe, Frederick was Antichrist, to all he was *Stupor Mundi*, and when he died, all the dark and secret and primitive beliefs of Germany, the forces of past paganism and future anarchy, were gathered up in the cult of his immortality. So firmly was it believed that he would come again, that once or twice he even conveniently appeared — until the imposture was discovered.

It is evident from this that some transformation of the legend was essential before it could be used for nationalist purposes. The transformation began early in the sixteenth century. The gradual solidification of nationalist sentiment rapidly put the international, extremely un-German figure of Frederick II out of fashion. Naturally, almost imperceptibly, Barbarossa slid into the vacant place. There was no denying that Barbarossa had all the solid German virtues so evidently lacking in his grandson: he had been a brave, bluff soldier, a strong ruler, a determined leader, and he had been intensely, and even consciously Germanic. Moreover, he was a sympathetic figure, undeniably '*gemütlich*', which could not be said of Frederick II. Rückert's too easily memorized — and, once memorized, unforgettable — quatrains have riveted him in the minds of generations of school-children.

But it is not in the selection and interpretation of national heroes alone that the German preoccupation with their past is most evident. It is recognizable in the too-careful preservation, the fossilization almost, of their ancient cities; it flaunted in Hamburg's huge Bismarck statue, regarded by patriotic citizens as the nineteenth-century equivalent of the ancient figures of Roland, which were the guardians of the old Hansa towns; it appeared in romantic guise in the lavishly restored or wholly rebuilt castles of the Rhineland; it shrieked in sheer madness from the pinnacled height of Neu Schwanstein. But all this is harmless and pleasant enough. No one with a taste for the bizarre can regret Neu Schwanstein and the faked castles have become as much a part of the landscape as the faked ruins of English eighteenth-century parks.

The danger comes only with the marriage of this innocuous play-acting, this national Bovarism, to the high technique of German scholarship. The Germans who have allowed themselves to be so bewitched by the romantic and the symbolic in their history also, and by an entirely separate process, gave birth to the most scholarly school of historians. The public mind is not very subtle; it cannot be expected to distinguish between attractive fable and actual fact. Still less can it do so if it is, as in Germany, desperately anxious that the fable should be fact, and generally befuddled by undiscriminating respect for authority and the printed word. German historical scholarship has gained, rightly, a very high reputation. The fruits of that reputation have been gathered in Germany by propagandists and irresponsibles. Rosenberg reaped where Ranke had sown.

The romanticization of German history has become a moral necessity for the maintenance of national self-respect. Light-hearted burlesquing of historical figures is rare and unpopular:

the 'de-bunking' of time-honoured heroes, which was no more than a refreshing exercise in other countries, was regarded with distaste and apprehension by the German public, so that historians and journalists who indulged in it gained more publicity than their research often deserved, and have many of them later paid for their disregard of national feelings in a manner out of proportion to the triviality of their work. It was significant of this same desperate preoccupation with their picture of the past that the Nazi Government made it an offence to 'traduce' the heroes of German history. German history, that sad and straggling tale of missed opportunities, division, frustration and defeat, varied by outbursts of desperate self-assertion, has got to be moulded into an image which is beautiful, coherent and *convincing*. One at least of the mad King of Bavaria's castles was designed, not by an architect, but by a scene-painter. At the risk of falling myself into the typically German fault of arguing from symbols, I am tempted to see in this a parallel to the weakness of German history as seen by the Germans. It is not founded squarely on fact and built for daylight; it is not architectural, but scenic.

THE ORIGINS OF GERMANY[1]

GERMANY has no frontiers; not only no natural frontiers but no self-explanatory political frontiers. The sea is the most effective of natural frontiers, with mountains — provided they are high and barren enough — a good second; rivers are a perennial source of dispute. It is, however, only necessary to look at the physical map of Europe to see that Germany has no evident framework. Geographically, there is no reason whatever for her existence. This is of course true of other countries: a nation is a political, not necessarily a geographical, entity, and although an indisputable boundary — like Great Britain's — is an advantage to the state as valuable as it is unusual, it is not indispensable to healthy growth.

The German problem was, however, intensified by the fact that this shapeless state of ill-defined and changing frontiers occupied a position of great economic importance. For centuries Germany dominated the overland trade routes and inland waterways of Western Europe. Her geographical position thus made of her a highway and a clearing station. While the commercial advantages were great the attendant political disadvantages proved to be even greater, for the interests of the people were drawn continually away from their own country, while the state lacked the necessary centripetal force to counteract the outward magnetism. The political development of Germany was, and is, out of step with her cultural and economic progress, a discrepancy which accounts for some of the contradictions in her conduct.

No other nation-state has changed its outline or shifted the balance of its governing authority so often as Germany. From the beginning her growth was haphazard. The upheaval of

[1] *The Geographical Magazine*, March 1944.

population in central Asia, which in the fourth and fifth centuries sent wave after wave of barbarian tribes to submerge the Roman Empire was slow to subside. Late comers found the civilized lands beyond the Rhine and the Danube already saturated. Germany, never, except in the south and west, more than an outpost of the Empire, now became the overflow. It was not a fortunate position, since pressure from the still nomadic tribes to the eastward continued long after further movement to the west had become impossible. Though it would be rash to determine the political characteristics of the numerous tribes from whom the future German race was to spring, it is worth noting that they were from the beginning a people of 'have-nots', a people forced to make do with the uncultivated wilds because the Goths, the Lombards and the Vandals had already occupied Roman Gaul and Roman Spain, Roman Italy and Roman Africa.

Whether the German character was indeed affected by this halting of their westward march, it is impossible to say. It was certainly affected in a negative manner by exclusion from the sphere of Roman influence. Some German historians have sought to trace throughout their country's history a sharp fissure between the western and south-western districts, along the Rhine and the upper Danube, which had belonged to the Roman Empire, and the regions in the outer darkness beyond. The distinction is not as clear as theory can make it appear, but it is certainly true that mellowing and beneficent influences in German history come more often from these regions, only to be dispersed in the bleak atmosphere of the northern plain.

No historical division is ever clear cut. There was no moment during the migrations when the last tribe squeezed itself into the pale of the Roman Empire and slammed the gates in the face of the next. Just as a fringe of Roman provinces in the west and south were ultimately to be part of Germany, so in the north we find one tribe half in and half out of the old Empire. The Franks gave their name to France; they also gave it to the province of

Franconia (Franken) in Germany. Had the Franks maintained their supremacy in the north-western section of Europe some kind of amalgamation between the romanized and the barbarian world might have been possible. They were a people who combined the enormous vitality of the barbarian with considerable adaptability and political instinct. Moreover, they produced several leaders of unusual ability and one of genius.

It is typical of the modern German attitude to history that they have rejected Charlemagne as a Frenchman. Charlemagne, the greatest of the Frankish kings, subdued the pagan Saxons along the Weser and thus laid the first outpost of Germany's eastward expansion, brought under control most of the disordered peninsula of Italy and revived in his own person the Roman Empire of the West. The lands which he ruled covered virtually the whole of modern France, about a third of modern Germany and something over half of Italy. It was not by any means an ideal state, geographically speaking. Italy at any rate was superfluous. Yet had this Franco-German Empire survived it must have been a consolidating force in Europe, controlling, as it would have done, the problematical German tribes. Its capital was situated significantly in the borderland between civilization and barbarism at Aix la Chapelle on the Rhine.

French and German historians alike trace the troubles of the Rhenish frontier to the disintegration of this Empire. It could not indeed have happened in a more unfortunate manner. Charles, the youngest of Charlemagne's grandsons, took most of modern France; Lewis, the second, known as Lewis the German, took the regions east of the Rhine; Lothar, the eldest and the stupidest, was given as narrow a strip of land as could possibly be carved out to include the two capitals of the Empire, Aix la Chapelle the administrative centre, and Rome the spiritual head. A ribbon of country, including most of the Rhine and the Alpine passes, was thus stretched out under the control of a weak ruler, at the mercy of two strong neighbours. Charles and Lewis made short work of Lothar. Over the spoils they came near to making short work of each other. No one can now exactly trace the battlefield of Fontanetum where they and their followers clashed, but it lies somewhere on the Flemish border ringed round with a hundred later battle-fields. Later they signed a treaty at a pivotal point on the new frontier: at Strasbourg. The debatable land had been created. As for Lothar, the only mark he left on Europe was the echo of his name in the province of Lorraine.

To the east of the debatable land Germany now began to develop as a separate enttiy. Here, far more strongly than within the ancient Roman Empire, tribal organization persisted as an undercurrent long after the tribes themselves had ceased to wander, and the country had been parcelled out under the feudal system. Traces of tribal law can be felt in the more brutal persistence of the blood-feud in Germany, and in the obstinate refusal of local privilege to be assimilated in any general system of justice. The occasional protests of criminals that they had a right to be tried by the law of their own people wheresoever in Germany their crime had been committed occur as late as the seventeenth century.

The most serious consequence of this failure of the nation to dissolve the tribe was its effect on German feudalism. In no other country of Western Europe did the barons attain to, or hold for so long, such far-reaching rights. In their struggle against the centralizing authority of a King or Emperor, they could rely on a support from their own people which had something in it of tribal devotion to a chieftain.

This powerful force increased the danger of disintegration which was always inherent in Germany's geographical situation. That part of Germany which had been part of the Frankish Empire covered roughly the western third of what is Germany to-day. Threatened and battered along its eastern edge by still unsubdued tribes, the German state grew at the expense of these neighbours. Building out into the uncivilized land first a bulwark, then a colony, then a further bulwark beyond, Germany stepped gradually eastward from river to river, from the Weser to the Elbe, from the Elbe to the Oder.

The migrations of peoples do not halt of themselves: when the Germanic tribes were brought up short in their westward march, the tribes in the rear were still pressing on. They continued to do so for centuries. The Germans, determined to hold at least what they already had, turned and fought. They are hardly to be blamed for that; where they made their error was in not knowing where or when to stop. They acquired simultaneously a panic-terror of encirclement and a highly aggressive frame of mind towards their neighbours. Insensibly the establishment of defensive lines towards the east, the gradual assimilation of heathen and barbarous peoples, the legitimate colonization of waste land developed into a policy of attack. The *Drang nach Osten*, which is so marked a characteristic of early German history, could only be checked by two things: a geographical barrier or a cultural barrier. But there is no geographical barrier on this eastern frontier; the monotonous sandy plain was an irresistible temptation.

It was a cultural barrier which stopped them. Quite suddenly the *Herrenvolk* came into collision with a civilization different from, but fully as advanced as, their own. This was the civilization of the Slav peoples. At this point colonization frankly gave way to aggression. Held back, defeated, they retired only to come again. The spontaneous need for expansion exhausted itself; it was kept alive by the policy of German rulers. In the seventeenth century the Czechs were ruthlessly subjected to Austria; in the eighteenth the King of Prussia and the Empress Maria Teresa divided Western Poland.

None of this, however, really gave to Germany frontiers which her rulers or her people regarded as satisfactory. Held up on the west because the Roman Empire had reached saturation point before they came, they were held up on the east because the Slav nations had stabilized and solidified in their rear. It is a fundamental maxim in German policy that existing frontiers are merely provisional.

While the frontiers remained thus wilfully undecided, the heart of Germany also failed to materialize. Anatomically speaking, the state was a monster. Conditions on the frontiers were partly to blame; German energies were dispersed round the perimeter instead of being concentrated at the centre of the kingdom. The power of the Emperors (German Kings had resumed the ridiculous title of Roman Emperor in the tenth century) was perpetually drawn off to the extremities of their kingdom, or more serious still, into Italy, where for centuries they sought to establish a true imperial authority.

In the centre, meanwhile, with its roads and its waterways, a commercial Germany of a different kind was developing independently of the imperial state. The same thing happened among the cities of the northern coasts whose commercial interests united them with England, France and the Scandinavian countries more closely than with the rest of Germany. Against a central government which was rarely more than a name, the active merchants of Germany soon established rights of their own. The free cities which were to be for centuries the true centre of German wealth and civilization contributed little or nothing to the idea of the German state. They made their own laws, existed independently of each other, levied their own taxes, even entered into their own agreements with foreign powers. Nor were the free cities the only independent powers in Germany. Some clever dynasts had succeeded in accumulating large provinces in their hands, shaping virtually independent states like Saxony and Brandenburg; but the pettiest barons and knights had often managed to establish an independence no less absolute. Goethe's Götz von Berlichingen boasted that he was dependent on no one but 'God, the Emperor and myself'. Dependence on the Emperor, it should be added, was theoretical.

The imperial dignity, faintly following the Roman model, was elective. Naturally enough the magnates responsible for choosing an Emperor were careful to avoid setting up a man or a dynasty stronger than themselves. As a result of the sudden switching from dynasty to dynasty in the Middle Ages, the German state had no chance to solidify (as the French did) about the personal lands of one family. The centre of gravity was constantly moving. We find it at Aix la Chapelle and generally along the Rhine during the ninth and tenth centuries, with a swerve eastwards to the Harz Mountains and Goslar in the eleventh, then farther south to Swabia with great assemblies at Bamberg under the Hohenstaufen. The Rhineland, with Speyer for the city of the Imperial Diet, was favoured by the earlier Habsburg; their later descendants converted Regensburg on the Danube into the official meeting-place, but used their own lands in Austria as the basis of their power, their capital at Vienna. Under the Emperor Charles IV in the fourteenth century Prague was to all intents the capital of the Empire; he himself, King of Bohemia by inheritance, partly Czech, and of the dynastic ruling family of Luxembourg, was perhaps the only Emperor whose private lands might have solved the German problem. He held as it were both frontiers — the Latin at Luxembourg, the Slav in Bohemia. A statesman of vision and patience, he might have achieved much had he had successors worthy of him. He, like Charlemagne, has a 'bad press' in Germany. Certainly his Empire would have solved the German problem by submerging the German centre between the French and Czech outer provinces.

In the sixteenth century the marriages of royal families began to make astonishing patterns in European geography, more particularly the marriages of the Austrian Habsburg. Charles V, on whom all the chief possessions of his family devolved, was elected Emperor in 1520. He controlled, besides Austria, Spain and the Netherlands. The Netherlands at this time were at least technically a part of the Empire, and their relations with the

THE ORIGINS OF GERMANY

Rhineland and North Germany were exceptionally close.
Charles V left them by will to his son, the King of Spain. This of
course did not in theory prevent them from being still a part of
the Empire; but imagine a situation in which an outlying province
of great importance, controlling the delta of the Rhine and the
Narrow Seas, is deliberately placed under the control of a foreign
power. Yet so ill-developed was Germany as a nation that
anomalies of this kind became in the ensuing century the rule
rather than the exception. We find the Kings of France, Sweden
and Denmark holding lands inside Germany, and German
princes holding lands outside it.

The Reformation, meanwhile, had divided the country against
itself. Both Protestants and Roman Catholics sought foreign
allies; in the first half of the seventeenth century the Empire
degenerated into little more than the fighting ground for all
Europe, as one foreign power after another was called in to settle
a problem which the German nation had failed to solve for itself.
Spanish, Swedish, Danish, Flemish, French and Hungarian armies
wasted the land for thirty years while German patriots vainly
longed for a saviour who would bring union to their distracted
country, and once or twice imagined that they saw him upon the
horizon.

There were in fact two possibilities during the war. The first
and that which came nearest to realization, was the amalgamation
of the entire country under Roman Catholic Habsburg sway,
ruled from Austria. The weakness and division of the northern
provinces and the genius of the imperial commander-in-chief
Wallenstein made the realization of this plan all but possible. The
state created would have pivoted on the river Elbe — the reason
for this being that Wallenstein was a Czech and moreover a man
of great personal ambition. He sought to build up a new political
entity based on an extension of his own country Bohemia, and in
particular of his own lands. When he had dispossessed the Duke
of Mecklenburg and carried the Austrian eagles to the Baltic

61

to lay siege to Stralsund, it looked as if the new state had been born.

At this moment the King of Sweden, Gustavus Adolphus, intervened. For the preservation of his own control of the Baltic it was evident that he must throw back the encroaching Habsburg state. But he was a man of profound religious convictions and of no less Napoleonic vision than Wallenstein. His plan for Germany was a northern confederation linked up with the Scandinavian powers, from which the Habsburg south could secede if it liked, a broken and emasculated fringe. His death in battle and Wallenstein's murder a year later put an end to both plans.

What actually happened during the Thirty Years War was the final destruction of imperial prestige — henceforward the Habsburg dynasty was to concentrate only on ruling its private dominions — and the collapse of the cities. The discovery of the ocean routes and the diversion of trade to all quarters of the globe had in any case robbed the free cities of their glory before the war. The war completed the process. There grew up instead the eighteenth-century Germany of small despotic principalities, principalities where the arts — on the French model — flourished, and which left monuments more beautiful, more civilized, more perhaps to our taste than the ornate Gothic of the cities. Such was the Zwinger at Dresden, or the noble episcopal palace at Würzburg with its lovely Tiepolo ceilings. Yet politically it was a vicious civilization, based on a class of subservient officials, and neither recognizing nor fulfilling any function in the political education of the people.

It was moreover a more feeble civilization nationally than any which had preceded it. The egoism and weakness of German rulers yielded the western frontier step by step to France, and the nineteenth-century neurosis about the Rhine was thus added to the others which had accumulated through the centuries. Yet this was something for which Germany had herself to blame.

The withdrawal of Austria from all pretensions to control the north made way for the unexpected growth of another power. Prussia-Brandenburg, in the seventeenth century the most contemptible of Germany's larger states, bankrupt, mortgaged and infertile, with a miserable capital city built of wood, soared into the ascendent under the rule of successive able and unscrupulous rulers. With an eye to essentials they cleared the Swedes off the Pomeranian coast and acquired the means to sea-power, solved the frontier question almost to their satisfaction by dividing up Poland with Austria and Russia, and gained both a strategic outpost to the south-east and invaluable mineral resources by annexing Silesia from a protesting Austria. The unification of Germany under Prussia in the nineteenth century was the logical conclusion. Taking advantage of the resurgent nationalism of the time and the evident incapacity of the other German states, Bismarck recreated the Empire with Prussia at its head. It was left, however, for Hitler, who combined in his person all the neuroses diffused among the German people, to realize the wildest of all Germanic imperial dreams, to re-incorporate Austria in the Reich and extend German dominion over half Europe.

The interaction of geographical position and political development has made of the German people a problem which all but defies solution. Their achievement in all spheres except the political has been creditable, in some cases outstanding. But it is the achievement of individuals, or at most, of small groups. They have not in the course of their history shown the least political insight. They are not merely bad neighbours, they are in the last resort bad citizens, lacking self-assurance and self-respect. For fifteen hundred years they have found themselves unable to accept their position in the European continent. What that position will be in future no longer rests with them.

MARTIN LUTHER[1]

THERE is no escape from Martin Luther. Whether we accept or reject him, admire or hate him, know him or are ignorant of him, we cannot evade the consequences of what he did to Europe, and through Europe to that great part of the world which has been affected by European thought. It would seem reasonable therefore to try to know him; yet of all the great controversial figures of history he is perhaps the most controversial, the most difficult to see with objectivity or precision. Since that week in April 1521 when at the Diet of Worms the obstinate monk faced the obstinate Emperor and the apparent unity of western Christendom cracked, it has been impossible to see Luther except from one side or the other of that great divide.

On the one hand there is the monumental pastor with the stubborn kindly face of German picture-book and German statuary, a foursquare giant caught for posterity in a perpetual utterance of his 'Here stand I, I can no other'. There is the opposing legend of the gross, lying monk gnawed with the egoist's unspeakable despair. There have been other fashionable versions — the German nationalist or the *petit bourgeois* ranged in his correct posture in the class war. Although none of these versions is wholly without foundation in the immense and inconsistent material which Luther's works provide, all are partial and therefore misleading, and there is not one among them all, which is, or will ever be, universally acceptable. What Martin Luther was has long been submerged in what he did, and what he did varies, more than the achievement of any other European, according to time, place and point of view.

Yet a periodic reassessment of Martin Luther is a necessity, not only in the pursuit of objective truth, here so elusive, but in order

[1] *Times Literary Supplement*, February 23rd, 1946.

to analyse and so to guide those powerful forces inherited from the past which live and work in the world to-day. The influence of Luther alike for good and for ill is not yet exhausted, and this moment, four centuries exactly since his death at Eisleben on February 18th, 1546, provides an occasion for examining afresh where we stand with him and he with us.

In the last fifty years two developments have deeply modified the conception of Luther. The first is the decline of religion as a controlling force in the western world and the second is the political career of Germany. It is the measure of the hold which Martin Luther still exercises over our imaginations that the blame for both these phenomena has been from time to time ascribed to him: for the first because he divided and — it is argued — therefore weakened the hold of organized faith, for the second because of his part in creating the German nation.

A distressful tract of history divides us from the time when Robert Browning's 'grand rough old Martin Luther' was the widely accepted view of the great Reformer in this country. The same tract divides us from the days when Carlyle rejoiced that the defeat of vapouring, vainglorious France had assured the happy ascendancy of sober, God-fearing Germany over our continent. The events which have shown Carlyle a mistaken prophet have not spared Luther's reputation, for the part which he played in creating the German nation was fundamental. 'There has never been a German', wrote Döllinger, 'who so completely understood, nay whose spirit I should say has been so completely imbibed by his nation ... The mind and spirit of the Germans were under his control, like the lyre in the hands of a musician.' Luther indeed, less than any other great figure which that nation has produced, can escape the consequences of having been a German; and the consequences to-day are no longer what they once were. Writing in 1900 Dr. T. M. Lindsay concluded his *Luther and the German Reformation* with the comfortable reflection that 'Luther is the type of the best German manhood, in his patient industry, his enjoyment of quiet home life among wife and bairns, his love of music and his power to kindle when occasion arises into the slow-burning fire which consumes opposition.' The modern school which sees in Luther Hitler's spiritual ancestor sees in him another type of German manhood. The difference between the points of view is not so much the result of intervening discovery and research as of the two world wars for which Germany is responsible.

The position of Luther has been more subtly compromised by the failure of the liberal experiment of the nineteenth century. In so far as Luther was accepted, however oddly, in the liberal tradition as one of the great liberators of the human spirit, the esteem in which he was held has wilted with the growing cynicism and desire for authority which characterizes this century.

With this shifting emphasis on the one hand, has gone on the other hand, an attack on Luther's obsequious political doctrines and on his personal subservience to authority. While one group of critics, yearning after the beautiful, disciplined and united Christendom which (on inadequate evidence) they imagine once to have existed, condemned him for its destruction, a second group, no less critical, condemned him for having given his large sanction to the authoritarian state. The man who had once been seen as the liberator of the human spirit was now more often represented as the man who had subjected spiritual to material values and the Church to the State. Matthew Arnold's penetrating phrase 'the greatest of the Philistines' was cheaply echoed by those who detected the Philistine but failed to see the greatness.

Luther thus faces the judgment of the twentieth century through a distorting perspective. The distortion must be corrected if we are to come to any clearer understanding of the man and his thought, and it is important that we should, for Luther has a part still to play in the regeneration of his own people, and in the struggle between material and spiritual values which has reached so acute a phase in our own time. It is indeed because our time differs fundamentally from his in the very premises on which human life and actions are based that so much misunderstanding of his teachings has arisen. Only by the effort to eliminate that misunderstanding and to see what Luther's theory meant in his own time, what was the balance and what the limitations of his outlook, can we once again grasp the heart of his message.

The elements which made up his volcanic power are not difficult to distinguish both from his own writings and from the comments of his contemporaries. He was a remarkable speaker, with a 'fine, distinct, pure voice', fluent, emphatic yet 'no great shrieker', possessed above all of the sympathetic power to fit his words to his audiences. The outspoken enemy of the pretentious, scholastic sermon, he believed in preaching to the humble in language familiar to them. It came to him easily, perhaps too easily, bursting forth in plentiful homely images, gross, earthy, graphic. He was one of the first great stylists of popular speech and he used the half-formed language of the people, with its immense potentialities of rhythm and colour and vehemence, with an artist's mastery. In his unashamed and unaffected handling of the ordinary words of ordinary men and women, no less than in the affectionate care which he took to appeal to lowly hearers he showed a democracy of the heart, in startling contradiction to his political teaching. It is for this reason above all that he has become so deeply a part of his country's tradition. He dominates a language in which there is no single influence comparable to that of his Bible, perhaps the most astonishing, impressive and highly personal translation ever compassed.

Martin Luther had further that colossal assurance without which no great Reformer can exist. True, he was subject to doubt, introspection and the dark torment of an egocentric bred in a strongly mystical tradition; but despair in him yielded always to the great overwhelming certainties. It would be vain to deny the ingenuousness of some of those certainties. The Scriptures were his measuring rod of the truth, but the interpretation, and in the end the translation too, was his. What he said of them, what he *made* of them thus became the truth. He rejected as inauthentic what did not suit him, the Epistle of St. James for instance, which carries his marginal note 'This is false'. Furthermore in that key passage of the Epistle to the Romans through which he himself had found his own great certainty — that salvation is by faith alone — he inserted in the German version that necessary missing word 'alone' to clinch the argument. 'It is true these four letters *sola* do not stand in the Latin and Greek texts', he defended himself, adding with some fierceness, 'and the blockheads stare at them like cows in front of a new gate.' Some might think the scholars, thus dismissed as blockheads, had the right of it, but Luther deeply convinced that he knew what St. Paul had meant, would not budge.

With this great certainty went also, undeniably, a great courage. Because the dangers he ran were less considerable than those braved by many other reformers we forget too easily that they were very great, and seemed so to Luther. His posting of his Thesis at Wittenberg and still more his burning of the Papal Bull were acts of defiance performed against a background of popular support. But the journey to face the Emperor at the Diet of Worms, notwithstanding Luther's popularity in Germany and the protection of the Elector Frederick of Saxony, needed real courage. John Huss, in circumstances not wholly dissimilar, had been seized and burnt at Constance, and Luther, only a few months earlier, had in the course of a deputation with Eck admitted that he did not believe certain of the opinions held by Huss to be heretical. Thus when he spoke of going to Worms to stand 'in the mouth of Behemoth between his great teeth and to acknowledge Christ' he was neither boasting nor jesting. The courage which he brought to that occasion must not be underestimated because the great teeth of Behemoth did not in fact gnash until he was well beyond their reach, and the imperial ban of the Empire was flung in vain against the defiant heretic monk already safe in hiding at the Wartburg.

Luther added to his assurance and courage an energy both of mind and body which gushed forth in a torrent of words, written, spoken, preached. He was well aware that his energy betrayed his scholarship; loose-knit and rough-hewn argument was the price he paid for readiness and vigour. In this he contrasted himself with the cautious Melanchthon. 'I hew the trees,' he said, 'Philip planes them.' Erasmus he described contemptuously as *Verba sine re*, but he described himself as *Res sine verbis*, seeing clearly how with him the impulse to action outran the slower processes of thought. He would have his ideas out and fighting before they were fully formulated as ideas. It has been well said of him that 'his words were half battles'. In that lay their strength while he lived and uttered them, and their weakness when exposed, in the static silence of the printed page, to unfriendly analysis.

In the early sixteenth century the spoken word was still as potent as the written. The sermon and the disputation carried a weight equal to and in some cases greater than that of the printed page. A whole orchestration of gesture and tone added to or modified a meaning and men were convinced by the ear in a fashion which is incomprehensible to us to-day. (The wireless will presumably in time redress the balance once more against the printed word: it is beginning to do so.) This change in emphasis has provided yet another subsidiary cause for the misunderstanding of Luther, whose subtler meanings were often and evidently associated with a rich expressiveness of voice and gesture and timing, which is wholly lost to us.

For this, among other reasons, too much has been made of that violence of expression which went with his stupendous verbal felicity and facility. Not that violence and coarseness are surprising in a sixteenth-century Saxon of peasant and mining stock, handling a vernacular which has at no period been remarkable for refinement. Words poured from him in torrents in the pulpit, at table, in religious controversy or domestic chatter; the crumbs alone, the Table Talk, fill six quarto volumes in the authoritative Weimar edition of Luther's works. This unexpurgated flood, bottled in season and out of season by scribes whose accuracy is not always beyond reproach, provides material enough for many portraits of Luther, including — with a little judicious selection — that of the brutal, mawkish, servile German of some modern critics. It is easy to generalize from selected instances where the material is so vast; it is easy to compare Luther's moods of bluster-ing defiance to his expressions of grovelling obsequiousness to princes, or to set against the savagery of his attack on the revolted peasants — that notorious passage in which he exhorted the princes to slaughter them like mad dogs — the tears he shed over a frozen violet. As there was inconsistency, and room for inconsistency, in Luther's powerful, productive mind, so in his character there was baseness. It was indeed an essential part of his greatness, the key to 'das Allgemein Menschlich' in him, which gave, and still gives, him his irresistible force. But to make by smart analogies and cheap juxtapositions a case against the whole character of Luther is merely misleading.

Few would now deny that Luther's political influence, on Europe and on Germany, was unfortunate. His innate conservat-ism, his deliberate subjection of the Church to the State and the doctrine of submission to the temporal power which was implicit in this, laid an effective foundation for the bureaucratic-auto-cratic state. It should, however, be remembered by those who blame him most vigorously for Germany's political failings that the first examples of the secular state to which he had given so great an impetus were outside Germany, in the France of Riche-lieu for instance. Moreover, the prevalence of his religious teach-ing in the Scandinavian countries does not appear to have had political effects in any way comparable to those it had in Germany.

The plain truth about Luther's political teaching is that time has played tricks on it for which he himself can hardly be held responsible. He could not be expected, living in an age which was profoundly religious, to foresee what would be the consequences of his political views in an age when the religious premises on which they were based had ceased to be effective. He accepted the temporal power with submissive acquiescence because the temporal power, being of this world, was of very little account. The spiritual, inner life of man, his only true life, was to be lived separately from his material life. Luther belonged heart and soul to an age of belief. He could hardly have imagined a world in which the spiritual life of man was very largely, and the next world totally, at a discount. His attitude to the State rested on his estimate of the relative importance of the temporal and the spiritual — an estimate so unflattering to the former that it was hardly worth more than intermittent and casual attention. There is in Luther's writing no clearly worked out theory, rather a series of impatient assumptions tending to the acceptance of the established order. This in the late Renaissance meant the acceptance of strong authority and, since religious sanction was necessary, the quasi-sanctity of the temporal power. God had set up the princes for this imperfect and transitory world. Luther's political beliefs must therefore be seen in strict relevance to his contempt for the world. It was, to him, the 'devil's inn' and he thought it to be approaching its last apocalyptic moments. It is fundamental to Luther's teaching that the temporal is not important. This attitude, pushed to a doctrine, has justified man's acquiescence in monstrous systems; but it has also produced a standard of Christian values outside and above all systems and provided the individual with a spiritual strength that no system of material politics can break. One point has in any case been insufficiently considered: did Luther's views of the State produce the notorious political weaknesses of the German people, or did the German people merely adapt certain aspects of Luther's teaching to suit circumstances which were by no means of his making?

What is needed to-day is to redress the balance of Luther's teaching more especially in Germany by a renewed emphasis on his religious experience. For here he taught a doctrine which is pure democracy. Here he escaped the restraining bonds of politics – necessarily perverting to religion since the Kingdom is not of this world. Here in this central core of his belief he is no longer the obsequious dependant of a temporal prince or the defender of property and law against revolt and anarchy. He is a man with a revelation.

His revelation, that the just shall live by faith *alone* (he must have his '*alone*' for it was part of his revelation, whether or not it was a part of St. Paul's), postulates the active responsibility of the individual. The act of belief has to be made; the change of heart is everything. Like all great revelations, his was a very simple one and not new, though to *him* it was new, and at once so personal and so overwhelming that, in the corrupt atmosphere of his time, he could feel only the necessity of making it general throughout the Church. He demanded for the whole Church as he knew it the change of heart, and certainly with Tetzel hawking Indulgences to a patter worthy of Autolycus a change of heart seemed overdue.

The Church met the challenge by manoeuvring him into heresy and demanding his retraction. He would not retract. So that instead of Reform there was a schism, and because there was a schism there was a weak young schismatic Church which had to grow (Luther had no choice) in the shelter of the temporal power. Hence the paradox: the subservience of the Lutheran Church arose from the bold assertion of the independence of man's soul which Luther had made. It is not the only paradox. It may be claimed that Luther completed the work of Hildebrand by shattering the Holy Roman Empire; and equally that he destroyed the work of the great medieval Popes by shattering the supremacy of Rome. It may be claimed that he was the architect of German unity and equally that he retarded German unity for centuries by creating the religious schism. But the greatest paradox of all was that his theory of man's inner responsibility towards himself and God led to the practice of his temporal subjection to the State which could alone guarantee the survival of the Reform.

A man with a revelation cannot be held down to the practical effects of his teaching in the narrow sphere of politics; and it is unjust to Luther to forget that his true province was not the State, but the soul of man.

THE CITY OF GOD [1]

My soul, there is a country . . .

SAINT AUGUSTINE died in his bishopric, the fortress town of Hippo Regius on the north coast of Africa, in the late summer of the year 430. Fifteen months earlier the Vandals, the most brutish of the barbarian tribes who had penetrated the crumbling frontiers of the Roman Empire, had leapt the pillars of Hercules into Africa. Masters of Rome's richest province and lords of the western Mediterranean they were soon, under their King, the ugly and crooked Gaisaric, to hold the Empire up to ransom. With the tide of this last calamity beating round the walls of his earthly city the Saint had died, leaving to his doomed contemporaries and to an unimaginable posterity his *City of God*.

The days of his life were the last of the Roman Empire. Born not long after the death of Constantine he had seen in his youth the deceptive stability established under Valentinian I and Theodosius. The elements of imperial order were still present and the furnishings of civilization were all about him: the baths and the hypocausts, the material wealth and physical comfort, the free food and the free entertainments. The world of learning flourished in disputatious vigour, its roots deep in the culture of centuries. But the Goths were crossing the Rhine and the Vandals the Pyrenees. There was pressure without, and within the paralytic rot — a parasite population and a rigid bureaucracy.

Christianity was the official religion of the Empire, but it was challenged by heresy and troubled by schism. Pagan learning and above all the fine teaching of the Neo-platonists dominated the schools. These were the influences which formed the mind of the young Augustine pursuing his studies at Carthage while the Goths shattered the imperial army and killed the Emperor Valens

[1] *Time and Tide*, April 20th, 1946.

at the calamitous battle of Hadrianople. This was in the year 378; nine years later Augustine was baptized. By the time he was consecrated to the see of Hippo in 395 the barbarian disintegration of the West was far advanced and the Empire divided between the feeble sons of Theodosius. In 410 Rome fell, to Alaric, King of the Visigoths. Such was the first century of official Christianity: a clouded opening.

In these dismal circumstances Saint Augustine began to compile his *City of God*. He had two motives for his writings. The first was to defend the Christian faith against pagan accusers who saw in the decay of the Empire the vengeance of the forsaken gods. The second was to raise above the wreck of a temporal Rome and beyond the dark horizon of his times the vision of the Heavenly City which has no end.

The first of these tasks, the refutation of paganism, seems remote from us; to Saint Augustine it was urgent. The struggle was a bitter one fought out inside the brain of every educated Roman Christian: the delights of poetry and the intellectual pleasures of a great culture came to these men almost with the odour of damnation about them. The beauty of classical literature, in which they had been bred, was a temptress beauty, and safety — for some of them at least — lay only in renunciation. This inner struggle, which Saint Augustine had himself experienced, reflects the vehemence and reality of the physical struggle which from time to time still came to the surface in the political world and which was always a latent danger. The apostasy of the Emperor Julian had occurred within Augustine's lifetime, and when Alaric was besieging Rome the senate had decreed the death of Serena, niece of the Emperor Theodosius, who, in a too outrageous display of her contempt, had helped herself to a necklace from the statue of the Mother of the Gods. Paganism was still powerful and seemed more powerful even than it was.

Saint Augustine thus appointed himself the defender of the True God against the dethroned population of false gods, and in chapter after argumentative chapter historically disproved the efficacy of Jupiter and his crew.

The contest in these terms seems unreal to us, and yet the struggle with false gods is perennial and may be in a more desperate state to-day than when Saint Augustine took up the challenge. For it was in the last resort the material values which Augustine challenged, the false faith which measures its gods by the worldly success they chose to bestow and offers material propitiation for material benefit. If we read for the pagan gods of the fifth century the gadget gods of the twentieth, the slogan gods, the scientific gods and the thousand superstitions of rationalism, the struggle is not foreign to us: only the terms in which it is couched. But the materialism of our time has not paganism's redeeming beauties and there is no Saint Augustine.

The second task which Saint Augustine undertook in *The City of God*, has however, the more immediate reality for us — the task of revealing the eternal kingdom beyond the earthly kingdom. Like Augustine we inhabit a threatened world; the threat being largely of our own making, is different in quality from the threat to the Roman order. Barbarian invasions and atom bombs have necessarily a different impact on human lives and the human mind. But both are unsettling.

Not that civilized society in the twentieth century is so near the abyss as it was in the fifth. Our world has not yet reached that visionary unreality, that hysteric oscillation between terrified excess and terrifying austerity, nor acquired the frantic appetite for public entertainment in the midst of public disaster.

Saint Augustine, citizen of the Roman Empire, belonged to its complex, huge, decayed fabric. It was the earthly city as he understood it. The medieval world with its feudal subdivisions, its territorial loyalties under the circumscribed authority of a Church whose boundaries were never so wide as those of the fallen Empire, would have been beyond his darkest imagining. Yet it was precisely this unimaginable medieval world which took Saint

THE CITY OF GOD

Augustine for its own, and which, through him, caught the great light of Plato, the only pagan who 'came near to the knowledge of Christ'. Otherwise his immense influence on the middle ages was one which might well have astonished him. From his well-furnished arsenal of learning and argument, ammunition was to be found for conflicts of which he had not dreamt. From the surge and movement of his style were to come, in echo and paraphrase, some of the loveliest passages in medieval Latin. The sea-beat of his

> Quanta erit felicitas, ubi nullum erit malum, nullum latebit
> bonum, vacabitur Dei Laudibus, qui erit omnia in omnibus?

melts into the bell-chimes of Abelard:

> O quanta qualia
>   sunt illa sabbata,
> quae semper celebrant
>   superna curia,
> quae fessis requies,
>   quae merces fortibus,
> cum erit omnia
>   deus in omnibus.

His ideas illumined Dante; his theories of the State sustained the established Church in Gregory VII and his theories of God undermined it in Wyclif and Luther. For if he believed that the earthly State was the outcome of sin, he also believed that God needed no mysterious intermediaries between himself and his creation. Strange that the Saint whose writings so dominated the middle ages should be in spirit so much closer to the Renaissance with its immense rediscovery of the human personality.

There is a satisfying basis of fact to the outlook of Saint Augustine: he understood the earthly city and indeed devoted much of his book to explaining it. After all it is a fact; it has to be lived in, whether it is the Roman Empire or some shield-clashing monarchy of the Franks or, for that matter, a Parliamentary democracy. Although it is the result of sin (Adam's sin) it is not necessarily bad. '*Set justice aside* and what are kingdoms but fair thievish purchases?' said Saint Augustine, thereby making it clear that justice is the essential. Nowhere does he suggest that it is the impossible. The earthly city can and should embody it. *The City of God* gives no countenance to the doctrine that the Christian is at liberty wholly to disregard the earthly city. On the contrary, in all those passages which explain the relations of the temporal with the heavenly kingdom — that is of the Christian with the State — there is a classic moderation.

> The heavenly city observes and respects this temporal peace here on earth, and the coherence of men's wills in honest morality.

The true Christian,

> being a citizen, must not be all for himself, but sociable in his life and actions.

And again:

> One may not be so given to contemplation that he neglect the good of his neighbour, nor so far in love with action that he forget divine speculation.

Only when there is evident conflict between the laws of the heavenly and the earthly city must the citizen of the latter take his stand against the temporary and temporal. This was the strength and comfort of Saint Augustine's message to a troubled world, for whatever befalls the earthly city the heavenly city stands firm.

Its citizens know no difference of language or nation; they come from the ends of the earth and are scattered over all the world; their common citizenship is in Christ. Their city was untouched by the Roman disaster; it has been seen in faith since then in every quarter of the globe, on the hills of China and in the jungles of Africa, and once with the brightness of revelation by a tinker in Bedford gaol. Disquieting doubt or dazzling vision, the faith is rooted deep in the hearts of men. It is this faith which to-day still nourishes the lurking doubt that antiseptics and full employment — good though these be — are neither man's ultimate goal nor his salvation and that, beyond the earthly city with its strivings and its power for good or for evil,

> If thou canst get but thither
> There grows the flower of Peace,
> The Rose that cannot wither,
> Thy fortress and thy ease.

GOOD COMPANY[1]

'ONE who is very much delighted with being in good company', wrote William Blake under a portrait of himself; and by 'good company' he did not mean merely good conversationalists. He used the expression in the wider sense from which our carelessness has narrowed it, the sense in which I once heard it aptly used to describe the novels of Scott — 'he is an author who always keeps good company'.

There is no doubt that we have failed lamentably of late years, both in literature and in life, to appreciate the value of good company. We have kept bad company for preference; I do not mean the company of the tough and the simple, which may be as good as any, but the company of the weak and the null. The high and the great qualities, or at least the expression of them, have been at a discount. There is something stoical and dramatic at first, something spuriously convincing in the reduction of all expressed feelings to a limited number of monosyllables, and coarse ones at that. But the adulation of the inarticulate leads in the end to the extinction of thought and feeling. If the supreme moments in life, whether of delight or anguish, are to be summed up in a grunt, it soon becomes impossible to distinguish the supreme moment from any other, or the moron from the genius.

This has been said before. The literary critics are all saying it, and the neo-romantic movement is already obediently at hand. But the suppression of thought and feeling has been more than a phase of literary fashion. In his *Critical Thoughts for Critical Days* Mr. F. L. Lucas regrets the times when men were nourished on Plutarch. This is a significant regret, for Plutarch stands for a whole theory of moral education. To be nourished on Plutarch was to be nourished on great deeds greatly told, on the grandeur

[1] *The Spectator*, November 20th, 1942.

of the past, not on its trivialities. For a long time now, historians have ceased to regard this moral strengthening as an important part of their office. It is interesting to know how people lived in the past, what they ate and how they paid for it; everyone should know what the conditions of the working classes were in the early nineteenth century, and the economic causes of the Hundred Years War are not to be neglected. Yet be the mind never so full of facts, the education of the heart is incomplete if no time has been left for Sir Philip Sidney at Zutphen. Until towards the end of the eighteenth century, history was chiefly regarded as the moralist's book of examples. Without wishing to relegate a highly developed science to that place again, one may wonder whether it fulfils so innocent or even so useful a purpose to-day.

More insidious and more distressing than the propagandist perversion of history — an old and inevitable evil — is the grey meanness which has enveloped the whole study. One purpose of historians is surely to provide us with that good company which is there for the seeking. 'Lives of great men all remind us ...' but they do nothing of the kind to-day, for we no longer read them, or at least not in that spirit. The good biographer is rare among us, the heroic biographer unknown. It was and is right to examine the sociological background and the economic structure of past society; but it is wrong in the process to lose sight of the great man and the great moment. We have more to learn to-day from the spectacle of a great man at a great moment than from any number of monographs on ancient wage-levels. For we have lost the art of living greatly, or assumed that it is no longer necessary to try.

The reasons for this flight from the heroic are evident; but they do not justify it. The social structure of Europe until very recently gave both the means of doing and of recording great deeds predominantly to one class. Those brightly illustrated children's histories which used to be in every nursery had a dozen valiant princes and heroic ladies for one Saint Joan. In our class-

F

conscious age this unintended emphasis on the prince or the
aristocrat became embarrassing; but it is futile to turn away from
great minds and great actions because irrelevant factors have given
them a snob value. More recently we have been afraid lest the
adulation of individuals should lead to the heresy of the *Führer-
prinzip* and have sought to merge greatness with the undistin-
guished mass. But democracy should lead to a higher, not a lower,
estimate of the individual, and what better standard of values
have we by which to judge merit than the study of great men?

For the company of the great is good company as Shakespeare
understood it, as Plutarch understood it. The past remains the
source from which example and precept can still be drawn. Here,
in spite of the debunkers and those who will spoil any good story
by pointing out that it is poorly authenticated, here is our example
and our hope. Men have been vile, stupid and self-seeking; but
they have also been noble, compassionate and enduring. History
has been lost too long in the desert of sociology and economics; it
has been poured into the filthy conduit of racial theory or solidified in the rigid economic mould. It has lost sight of the individual
and in so doing has forfeited its moral influence and more
generous purpose. It should be the historian's business not to belittle but to illuminate the greatness of man's spirit.

MISS MANGNALL OF THE QUESTIONS[1]

PRINCESS ANGELICA, only daughter of King Valoroso XXIV of Paflagonia, it will be remembered by addicts of *The Rose and the Ring*, was held up as an example to idle pupils by their governesses. 'She could play the most difficult pieces of music at sight. She could answer any one of Mangnall's Questions!' Soon the Paflagonian schoolroom will be the last niche in the temple of fame left to poor Miss Mangnall, later editions of whose valuable work, limp from the thumbing of long-dead governesses, are sometimes to be found in the fourpenny boxes in the Charing Cross Road. Her book, privately printed in 1800, was later acquired by the enterprising firm of Longmans, ran into revised edition after revised edition, and became the mainstay of the pre-Victorian and early Victorian schoolroom. And what an admirable mainstay it was. A copy came into my possession from the unworthy source mentioned above — fourpennyworth, as I lightly assumed, of innocent amusement for a short train journey. I underestimated Miss Mangnall. Not only was I put to shame by my own ignorance — did I know that Fuller's Earth was an 'unctuous kind of marl', or even that gratitude was the distinguishing virtue of the Egyptians? — but I was filled with nostalgic admiration for the balance, the logic, the firm and reasoned outlook of this astonishing lady. With far more confidence would I place Miss Mangnall's *Questions* in the hands of 'the young person' than many a modern work sterilized by child-psychology and embellished with the self-consciously ingenuous pictures that children are now supposed to like — as if every right-minded child did not immediately prefer *The Boyhood of Raleigh* by Sir John Everett Millais.

The fact is that Richmal Mangnall, born according to tradition in Manchester in 1769, and for many years head-mistress of

[1] *Time and Tide*, May 2nd, 1942.

Crofton Hall in Yorkshire, belonged to the Age of Reason. Her face, under the neatly fastened turban, is that of a pre-eminently sensible woman: shrewd eyes, kindly mouth, open features. Her *Questions*, which are chiefly devoted to History and Antiquity with a brief section on Astronomy and General Subjects, imply an exalted philosophy of life. Black is black to Miss Mangnall and white is white, the colour being irrevocably determined on the highest moral principles. Her prejudices, which are many and unconcealed, arise from high-mindedness, if a little also from ignorance. Believing what she did of the Hierarchy, the Inquisition and the Mendicant Orders — which 'prevented the dawning light of the thirteenth century from penetrating the regions of darkness' — how could she think well of the Church of Rome? She had none of that unnerving impartiality which in more recent handbooks cloud the youthful mind with doubt. Her later editors and revisers maintained, together with her dignified prose, her upright prejudices and her exemplary freedom from subservience or hypocrisy. To the last Mangnall's *Questions* spoke with Johnsonian authority and fearlessness, the voice of the eighteenth century ringing out over the nineteenth.

As a guide in politics and morality she was, if conventional, yet extremely sound, though here and there infected a little with a plutocratic bias. When asked whether prosperity or adversity most tried the human soul, her pupils were to reply: 'Prosperity, as that condition affords the opportunity of proving either its true greatness or the vices which may be concealed in it.' Lucky hand-loom weavers, fortunate labourers of Speenhamland! Their souls were spared the supreme test. But no fault can be found with her answer to the question, 'What is true glory?' Her definition is precise: 'Active benevolence, fortitude to support the frowns of fortune, evenness of temper in prosperity, patience in afflictions, contempt of unmerited injuries; this is virtue, and the fame of virtuous actions can alone be called true glory.' Politically she was a firm believer in the 'superior excellence' of the English constitution, stalwart in her defence of freedom of conscience, and, as the years went by and new editions appeared, proud of her country's claim to have 'struck off the chains that galled the African slave'.

Nothing was omitted from her scrutiny. Each English reign is credited with its 'principal inventions and discoveries'. The use of the globes was introduced under King Edward I, a period at which 'it is remarkable that wine was sold as only a cordial, in apothecarys' shops'. Starch and the horse-guards come under King Henry VIII, speaking trumpets under Cromwell; the Northern Lights were first observed in the time of King George I.

She was wonderfully absolute too in her classifications. 'Name the four most ambitious men in Rome?' she asked: 'name the four most temperate Romans? Name the three most luxurious?' There is no arguing about the answers, no protesting that Catiline may have been more ambitious than Marius, or Caesar more luxurious than either. The abominable 'Sylla' figured in both the first and third category. Honour, however, where honour is due. 'The Duke of Wellington was equally eminent in the senate and in the field, sternly upholding the line of duty without fear or favour. It has been said of him that he made the service of public life more masculine: he rebuked by his conduct restless vanity, and reprimanded the morbid susceptibility of irregular egotism.' In sentences like these Miss Mangnall's English achieves lapidary perfection. Nelson, for instance ... 'after hoisting the English flag over the united fleets of France and Spain, closed his glorious career in death; his grateful country rewarded him with substantial favours while living, and has since raised monuments of brass and marble to a memory more lasting than either'.

Miss Mangnall's scrupulous use of words gives distinction to even the commonest questions. 'Whence are cocoa-nuts procured?' she asks, and not, as you or I would, 'Where do coconuts come from?' thus committing an assault on grammar and condemning one of the pleasantest words in the language, the charming 'whence', to undeserved neglect. But although sensitive to the beauties of literature, Miss Mangnall and her editors were sound on decency. The works of Rabelais, 'a Frenchman', 'were greatly deficient in that delicacy without which genius may sparkle for a moment, but can never shine with pure undiminished lustre'.

The spacious dignity of many of the answers must have enriched the common vocabulary of generations of young English ladies, while doubtless making Miss Mangnall's name hateful for ever in their ears. Like many of the best educationists she was more concerned with the teacher than with the pupil: her manual was designed to preserve the energies and the temper of the harassed governess while supplying her deficiencies of education and character. The first edition of the *Questions* is a pocket volume which could be slipped into reticule or work bag, and unobtrusively propped on the knee beneath the edge of the schoolroom table. Instruction and crochet might thus proceed simultaneously. How many oppressed gentlewomen, from 'poor Miss Taylor' in the elegant parlour at Hartfield to the tameless Brontës in the stuffy schoolrooms of the Yorkshire gentry, as they sat down to face lethargic or hostile pupils, must have breathed a silent thanksgiving for the gift of a strength not their own.

ASPECTS OF POLITICS[1]

I

'UNLIMITED power is apt to corrupt the mind of those who possess it', said the elder Pitt. He was not, presumably, the first person to notice this phenomenon, and he was certainly not the last. Lord Acton's more epigrammatic version has become a cliché of our times. 'Power tends to corrupt, and absolute power corrupts absolutely. Great men are almost always bad men.'

Pitt's statement pleases me better if only because it does not so readily lend itself to quotation in and out of season. Lord Acton was too wise and too widely informed a man to have built as much on that quotation himself as has been built upon it since. He did not — if I remember rightly — suggest that power was the only corrupting influence, a suggestion which on the strength of his dictum we now hear inferred or asserted in the strangest quarters.

Yet surely the most cursory glance at the world about us shows that powerlessness is at least as demoralizing as power. More men are undermined by frustration than by success. 'Since we cannot attain to greatness,' wrote Hazlitt, 'let us have our revenge by railing at it . . .' We are more subtle to-day. How comforting is the smug reflection that since power corrupts, we, who have none, are not corrupted. But that is not what Lord Acton said.

The rise and fall in the popularity of certain quotations is an index to some of the currents in the thought of our time. Disillusion with, and suspicion of, power are not in themselves unhealthy things. Rather the reverse. But human associations of thoughts are never simple, and the overstated suspicion of power joins in our own time with another influential current —

[1] *Time and Tide*, August 4th, October 21st and November 4th, 1945.

the suspicion of motive which has come to us with the diffusion of certain psychological truisms.

On the one hand we accept the dictum that power corrupts and is therefore bad (and add joyfully 'All great men are bad', for we shall never be great ourselves and this gives a kind of merit to our failure). On the other hand we accept a general, and in itself sound, theory that all motives are corrupt, springing from subconscious causes over which man's control is limited by his ignorance. But the human being is built with a curious inability to apply a general truth to his own case. Self-deceived and corrupted motives invalidate the actions of other people – or in politics, of the other party. They have nothing to do with our own.

These are overstatements, debating points if you will. Yet the presence of these two currents in the general thought of our day is undeniable and their confluence has produced a third and more important tendency. Suspicion of power and suspicion of motive, valuable if held in control, paralyse all human action if they themselves take control. They breed disillusion with that active and essential part of man's life which we call politics. And the politics of our time certainly give ground for this disillusion – though not more than the politics of many other times in the unquiet history of our race.

Wars and aftermaths of wars are not edifying; elections are not edifying; political trials are not edifying. Man as a political animal appears mean, vindictive, ambitious, self-interested and distressingly ingenious at shifting the blame. All over the world we see him parading his deplorable weaknesses, we forget how heroic a figure he cut – was it yesterday?

All this provides excellent excuses for disillusion. It becomes almost a virtue to dismiss politics with a shrug of the shoulder as a dirty business, a vulgar and self-interested scramble for power. Now is the time for all good men emphatically not to come to the help of the country. Now is the time for seclusion and the monastery.

At certain moments in the history of our civilization there has been a paramount need for this retirement of the good. Thus only did Saint Benedict and his monks among the crags of Italy preserve the moral code of Christendom from the collapse of the Roman Empire. But our state has not yet reached that extremity — not quite. Nor are the majority, if indeed any, of our disillusioned of the stature of Saint Benedict. It is absurd to confuse a gentlemanly distaste for the vulgarity of the political scene with a call to abandon the world.

The anti-politicals of our time have with few exceptions no intention of retiring to monasteries — or even to California. The lofty eminence from which they condemn the political world exists largely in their imagination, for they continue to live in and on that society which the politicians are doing their best to sustain or destroy. And in so far as they and we live in that world I do not see by what right we can dissociate ourselves from its political life. Corrupt motives are not the monopoly of politicians or businessmen — though reading the literature of disillusion would lead one to think so. Disillusion itself breeds corruption of motive, and men may withdraw themselves from the duties and responsibilities of their time for reasons no less corrupt than those for which other men shoulder them. The danger of the anti-political teaching of our day is that it encourages, in our tired and irreligious society, not saintliness but *fainéantise*. We forget in the smug condemnation of the political world that its standards depend, and always will depend, on the moral quality of the men who go into it. It is true that saints are rarely found in politics. But it does not follow that only scoundrels are.

'Power to do good', wrote Francis Bacon, 'is the true and lawful end of aspiring, for good thoughts, though God accept them, yet towards men are little better than good dreams except they be put in act; and that cannot be without power and place, as the vantage and commanding ground.' As a statement of the practical view of the political problem, that cannot be bettered, and to insist on Bacon's own too patent imperfections both as man and statesman, would be beside the point.

In an imperfect world we cannot afford to insist on absolute standards. Only very rarely have successful men positively disliked being successful and they have not always been better men on that account. Personally I should feel comparatively little confidence in a Prime Minister who did not evidently rather enjoy the job. No one pretends that enjoying power is good in itself, but it is a necessary concomitant of the temperament which seeks expression through action, that is through power. It is a weakness rather than a vice, and by no means the monopoly of the politicians.

Before the psychological fashions of our time had made every one suspicious of motives, before all good men were shown up as bad men cleverly disguised, our grandfathers very properly believed that the desire to do good might be an important element in deciding a man on a political career. We have grown so clever to-day that we know this desire to do good is only a polite word for power lust, mere humbug.

Humbug which could abolish the slave trade, free America, reform the prisons, release the children from the mines and factories, and fight with dogged and often unrewarded persistence the hundred battles which are still going on to-day was not without value to the human race. Better perhaps a little humbug than a vast cynicism.

II

About fourteen years ago in a train in Russia I was informed by a young student that history did not begin until the French Revolution. The view was evidently a simplified one put forward for my benefit and has been as far as Russian doctrine is concerned very much modified of later years. Dmitri Donskoi and Ivan the Terrible — not to mention Peter the Great and several other heroes of recent Russian monster historical novels – were all a long way pre-Revolution. But let that pass; the grain of truth behind my Russian student's statement is one that we must reckon with in our time.

What happened at the Revolution was that the concept of 'the people' became for the first time vital. Earlier ages, it is true, can show a fair number of statesmen and thinkers for whom 'the people' did in fact mean something fully realized and understood; but as a political force the idea lacked reality. 'The people' figured for the most part as a catch-phrase, sometimes meaning only the upper classes of society, sometimes an ill-defined and despised mob. Spasmodic popular risings there had always been, Jacqueries and Peasants' Revolts or such narrower outbursts as the Gordon Riots. But 'the people' (almost always 'the mob' when they expressed themselves in this way) exercised no sustained and hardly even a spasmodic influence on political events.

It is the undoubted and revolutionary contribution of the last century to have brought 'the people' – not as a mere concept but as a force – into a dominating place in politics. We live in a period in which democracy is for the first time a practical possibility. Cynics have pointed out that it is also the period in which a war fought to make the world safe for democracy was followed within a generation by its widespread disappearance.

But Fascism is the disease of democracy; therein lies its peculiar danger and the explanation of its virulence in our time. It appeared in its most violent forms among those populations which were least politically adult, that is, whose people had had least preparation for the opportunity when it came to them. It developed forms which, for all the general resemblance of the doctrine, had strongly marked characteristics derived from the nation wherein they grew. But the study of the peculiar national, political or economic conditions which gave rise to the particular forms which we have recently crushed in Europe must not be allowed to blind us to the fact that it is a disease to which every modern democracy is subject. The body politic of every democratic country is vulnerable.

The casual use of such words as despotism, dictatorship, tyranny — all of them dating from pre-democratic periods — confuses the issue. Fascism, though it leads in the old Machiavellian way by craft and conquest to the elevation of one man or one small group, can only succeed by first seducing 'the people'. The ingenious propaganda mechanism by which alone it survives is evidence enough of this. 'The people' may be silenced, intimidated and crushed, but they must also in large measure *believe*. *Credere, obbedire, combattere* as every other blank wall in Italy proclaimed. And it would have been an interesting experiment to count, during a short walk in any German town, how often the word *Volk* winked alluringly from the political hoardings.

The special constitution of a nation may be more or less subject to the Fascist disease but it is folly in the critical age through which we are living not to recognize that any democratic constitution provides by its very nature a breeding ground for its germs. Democracy, like the human organism, carries within it the seed of its own destruction. The defeat in arms of the two nations which were Fascism's prime advocates was a necessary operation, but does not in itself guarantee any other nation against an outbreak of the disease. If democracy is to survive we must diagnose the cause and find the prophylactic for Fascism.

The danger lies in the still incomplete conception of 'the people'. On Christian and liberal principles, the emergence of 'the people' as a political force was a great advance, although there were aesthetic by-products of oligarchic and aristocratic society which we shall never see again and which are a permanent loss to society. They would be too dearly bought back at the price of the *ancien régime*; that I suppose no liberal thinker can deny. Moreover, they could not at our present stage of society be bought back, for the choice is no longer between popular and aristocratic government, but between the rule of the people as we understand it in this country and the perversion of democracy which for lack of a better word we call Fascism. In politics it is impossible to undo the centuries and we must face the problems of our time as we find them.

The weakness from which democracy — the government of the people — suffers is a weakness of definition. What are 'the people'? The answer, thoughtfully given, is of course that they are the whole of society (not merely one class — a common error this), but — and this is more important — that they are a great number of separate entities, each one having a separate birth and death and an astonishingly large number of quite peculiar characteristics.

When politically conscious society was confined within small compass it would never have occurred to anyone to obscure the private entity of each of its members. It is because of the vastness of modern democracy that party and class have been given a higher value than the individual. Since 'the people' became a force in politics the individual has been progressively submerged; it is the natural outcome of the increase in the population of the political world. Our narrow imaginations cannot conceive of the mass in terms of individuals, and the first effect of giving every man his right to a say in his political fate has been the removal from him of his identity as a man. He becomes a party-member, a worker, an Aryan or what you will.

This is the subversive tendency which must be overcome in our time if democracy is not to perish. We must find means to extend our political imagination so as to reduce the necessity for simplification and grouping. We must above all find means to eradicate in men and women the primitive fears which make them seek refuge in groups and herds, preferring the cosy irresponsibility of the mass to the responsible loneliness of the individual.

European culture as we know it rests on respect for the individual. That respect has in our time dwindled until hardly even lip service to the old idea is left. If democracy is to survive, if the State is to be the instrument of man, not man of the State, respect for the individual must be imaginatively increased and extended as never before. Only in this way — and not by the organizing of parties and shouting of slogans — can the body politic be immunized against Fascism. But it is easier to diagnose than to prescribe and indeed the chief reason for the sickliness of most bodies politic is the failure of political theorists — even the most experienced and the wisest — to find the solutions to the problems they set forth.

The entry of the people into the field of effective government has altered the face of the political world and should alter it for the better. So at least the Levellers and the Idealists (of whom I count myself) have hoped for centuries. Meanwhile there is still the dangerous corner of Fascism, of the wholesale deception and enslavement of the people, to be turned. The person most to be feared in modern society is the Common Man. He is, like the Average Man, the Economic Man, and a host of his prede-cessors, a figment of the imagination. It does not make him any the less dangerous. Indeed, in some respects, it makes him, as an idea, even more dangerous.

The essential thing about each one of us is that we are unique. However mass-produced our fashions and ideas, however stereotyped our accents, no two human faces are exactly alike, no two human handwritings are indistinguishable, and — to the accurate listener — no two human methods of speech are identical — the word arrangement, the attack, the particular selection of threadbare idioms from the common pool remains individual. Different experiences differently accepted have differently shaped and carved each home-going face in the crowded train. 'I know nothing after all so real or substantial as myself', said Lord Shaftesbury at a period when life, if more callous for some, was less exhausting for all. Under the pressure of our own times it is only this confidence in our own identity which enables us to navigate at all the rapids of our world.

But there is a parallel instinct which makes most of us, while propelling our little skiffs more or less inexpertly along, seek to join up for company with the thousands of other little skiffs shooting the rapids in the same direction. The success of the human being in negotiating these rapids depends on the success with which he can reconcile and combine the necessary egoism and the necessary desire to move with the herd. In different societies and at different epochs the balance between the two has been differently held; a smaller deviation will serve to make a man an eccentric to-day more than it did in the eighteenth century. (Is there perhaps something a little wistful in the prevalent vogue for studying the eccentrics of the past?)

But to come back to the Common Man. He does not exist in the flesh. And no one, I imagine, so interprets the phrase as to mean that in this century of the Common Man we are all to aim at a certain dead level of ordinariness. On the contrary, we all ought to know by this time that the Common Man is a fine fellow. Has he not just won the war against Fascism? And yet ... When the great names are purposely omitted from a nation's expression of thanks to its saviours, there must surely have been a number of common men (without capitals this time) who paused to wonder whether Field-Marshal Montgomery had not perhaps contributed rather more to the total result than each of them.

This is in no sense to minimize the joint effort of a whole people, still less the countless personal efforts which added up (fantastic addition) to the united effort. The war against Fascism has been won — hitherto — by the Common Man as no earlier war in history has been so won. But what inspired these individual efforts? What kept the telephone operator at her task as the bombs whooshed down and nerved the bank clerk to tackle the incendiary bomb, and made thousands, even millions, of men and women carry for six years burdens of work and worry far beyond their strength? Surely it was something very different from a belief in the Common Man. It was the desire to be the Uncommon Man, or, call it by its old name, the hero.

Centuries of moral teaching have held up for our admiration certain high individual examples of conduct. The hero is a figure which it is still fortunately impossible to escape. He dominates our earlier literature, he prances across the old history text-books. He is still to be seen riding or meditating or gesturing in public squares. (True that investigation of his identity may be baffling. 'Sir Francis Hotchkiss, Bart., 1804-1882'; what can be made of that?) All the same the great man was — and is — there, to be respected, to be emulated, an example. And the Common Man rose, and rises, to the great occasion when it comes, because for centuries all the moral teaching he has had has taught him to aspire — not to ordinariness — but to greatness.

But the trend of moral and political teaching in our own time is away from individual greatness and example. Since the common people came into their own, emphasis on uncommon people has come to be regarded as bad taste. The tendency is a necessary part in the process of democracy, and without some temporary over-emphasis on 'the people' in the part of hero the balance, once too sharply tilted in favour of the individual, could hardly have been redressed. I do not myself forget the day when I stumbled on to those lines of Auguste Barbier on the Revolution of 1830 —

> La grande populace et la sainte canaille
> Se ruaient à l'immortalité . . .

and a flaming Red Dawn for some time afterwards blinded my eyes to any heroism other than that of 'the masses'.

But the balance can tilt too far, for on the whole crowds are rarely more admirable (and frequently less so) than individuals. If the Common Man becomes the exemplary type, all aspiration ceases and the Common Man will no longer be admirable. The saving grace, and also the danger, lies in the fact that no teaching and training can ever eradicate the desire to admire and to aspire which exists in every human being. It must find its outlet. And this brings the argument back to the starting-point; for if with the most laudable democratic intentions we play down the Great Man, whether in our own time, or in the records of the past, something else will usurp that necessary place. The film star, naturally; or the types portrayed by the film star, the gangster and the gangster's moll. But all this, though significant, is not so harmful as the political outcome of this levelling of greatness. What standards of choice will be left to us? What kind of windbags and nonentities will be able to deceive us? If this is really to be the Century of the Common Man we may expect a flood of pinchbeck dictators.

For the truth is that men do not desire to be the Common Man any more than they are the Common Man. They need greatness in others and the occasion to discover the greatness in themselves.

TWO PAINTERS

I. SIR ANTHONY VAN DYCK[1]

SIR ANTHONY VAN DYCK died in England in December 1641, where, for nearly ten years, he had made his home. It was that gloomy winter when the tension between King and Parliament had all but reached breaking-point and Van Dyck's death appositely underlined the close of a period.

It had been an interlude for gracious action and diffused intellectual endeavour, when Inigo Jones designed the royal masques and Wenceslas Hollar etched the capital and taught the royal children to draw, when William and Henry Lawes composed their delicate airs and the number of young poets self-consciously writing was probably greater than at any time until our own. The young men whose attenuated faces Van Dyck had painted would improvise no more verses in the gardens of Whitehall, would experiment no more in their private laboratories with alchemy and magnetism, nor stroll on the lawns at Compton Wynyates or Great Tew talking of philosophy and the constitution. The bitter flood of political conflict, dammed up for ten years, was soon to obliterate the precocious flowers of the Caroline Renaissance.

Van Dyck had settled in London in 1632 and had been from the outset the darling of the Court, the King having a special landing stage constructed the more conveniently to reach his studio from the Thames. The painter lived beyond the precincts of the Puritan and disapproving City, in Blackfriars, a district wealthy, cosmopolitan and just a little disreputable. His elegant house, soon a rendezvous of society, was at one time ruled by the handsome demi-mondaine Margaret Lemon, at another by pretty Anne Carlisle, the miniaturist. The King himself gave a kind of

[1] *Time and Tide*, December 6th, 1941.

left-handed approval to this attachment, since he once presented
Sir Anthony and Mrs. Carlisle with five hundred pounds' worth
of ultramarine for their joint use. Afterwards the painter decided
to settle his affairs more suitably, and laid all but successful siege
to a nobleman's widow, Lady Stanhope, only to lose her at the
last by ungallant insistence on payment for her portrait. Soon
after the Queen selected from her household a nobly born but
suitably impoverished bride, Mary Ruthven. But this was
towards the end of Van Dyck's career, when the informality of his
earlier days — he had once made a habit of asking sitters to stay
and dine with him so that he might study and sketch expressions
as they talked and ate — had given place to the business-like
methods of a fashionable practitioner. Sittings in his last phase
were for an exact hour, at the end of which Sir Anthony cour-
teously bowed the client to the door, while efficient servants
cleaned his brushes and brought out the canvas and special
palette for the next sitter.

Van Dyck's English period was the most prolific in his career:
a century later Walpole declared that his 'works are so frequent in
England that the generality of our people can scarce avoid
thinking him their countryman'. Since Walpole's time the
collection of paintings in public galleries and of facts in reference
books have dispelled this genial intuition. No one to-day thinks
of Van Dyck as an Englishman. We compare him learnedly with
Rubens in whose studio he worked as a young man; we pursue
the development of his style and distinguish between the first and
second Flemish periods, the Italian period and his last, declining,
English period. Yet if we assess him the more justly as a painter
we miss one aspect of the truth. The fashionable portrait painter
stands next only to the diarist as the recorder of a period; and in
Van Dyck's age there was no diarist to compete with him. His,
above all, was the imaginative sympathy which created our
nostalgic vision of that lost decade.

Born of prosperous middle-class parents in Antwerp, highly

trained in the professional technique of his art, Van Dyck would not at first seem to be the most sympathetic interpreter of the aristocratic dilettantism of the 1630s. But he had the successful portrait painter's essential gift, and saw men, with few exceptions, as they liked to see themselves. In Italy he had transformed the effete members of a stagnant society into figures solid with the consciousness of great traditions: in Flanders he gave an air of prosperous resolution to anxious statesmen and hard-pressed burghers. So in England, in the entr'acte of the great constitutional drama, he painted the nobles and their ladies with the gracious serenity of a land lapped in unending peace. The inhibited, adenoidal face of King Charles, unflatteringly rendered by Mytens, was transfigured by Van Dyck's hand with indefinable spiritual grandeur. The pompous Arundel became an elder statesman, the harassed Strafford a fortress of power, the crafty Pembroke a wise Ulysses, and eligible young peers — Carnarvon, Wharton, Digby — achieved a grace that flesh alone could never simulate.

Van Dyck, as an eighteenth-century writer expressed it, 'was the first painter who e'er put ladies' dresses into a careless romance'. But 'careless romance' was the mood of all his sitters, men and women alike: one recalls the artfully tangled curls of Lord Wharton, the clothes, all slashings and slits, of Lord John Stuart, through which lawn and lace profusely tumble, the trailing sashes, the lace-edged breeches, the wrinkled boots of soft leather. Did fashion ever more accurately mirror a period of grace and fantasy, of talk and postponement?

Yet it is in the rendering of a face or the choice of an attitude, rather than by details of dress, that Van Dyck built up our vision of the period. How far is this picture true? It can be modified by comparison with the work of other painters, with the etchings of Hollar and Faithorne, with the monumental sculpture of our churches. It must be modified in the light of history, for these gentle-faced sitters, Cavalier and Roundhead alike, were soon to face each other in uncompromising war: they always had it in them to be what they became in the next disastrous decade. The tranquillity of England in the 1630s, like that of the 1930s, was self-imposed illusion. Van Dyck enshrined the illusion for posterity.

II. THE ENGLISH TINTORET

At Oxford, opposite St. Mary's Church in the High, with its new porch on barley-sugar columns and Our Lady in a baroque attitude, the painter William Dobson improvised a studio during the noisy years of the Royalist occupation. Sociable, gifted, extravagant, the painter flickers briefly across the darkening scene of England's Civil War, the most striking of Van Dyck's followers and the most talented English painter of the seventeenth century. Elevated to the courtier's rank as groom of the privy chamber, he had succeeded his friend and discoverer Van Dyck as sergeant-painter to King Charles I. As Van Dyck has fixed for after ages the visual graciousness of the Cavalier summer, so it was Dobson who recorded their stormy sunset. His is the harassed King, with thinning hair and sagging features, dictating, buff-coated, to the stout and unperturbed Sir Edward Walker seated at a drum for a table. His is the sensitive, saturnine Rupert, handsome, haughty and strained. His is the upward tilted head of Montrose, the oblique studio light striking downwards on open forehead and obstinate jaw.

Temperamentally the painter was not unsuited to the uncertain time which saw his brief apogee. He came of the hanger-on class, poised always uncertainly between opulence and bankruptcy. His father, a St. Alban's man of some little fortune, had been a favourite of Francis Bacon and a dilettante of the arts, or at least of architecture, for Aubrey tells us that Bacon's house at Gorhambury, that 'most ingeniously contrived little pile' was built with his advice and help. Bacon rewarded him with a civil service sinecure, the mastership of the Alienation Office. The post availed the luxurious Mr. Dobson little, for as Aubrey concludes 'he spent his estate upon woemen' and thus 'necessity forced his son William Dobson to be the most excellent painter England hath yet bred'. Necessity was apparently for once the mother not merely of invention but of genius.

William Dobson was born in 1610, but it was not until the later 1630s that he began to attract attention. The facts of his early career rest on hearsay. He seems to have been at one time a pupil of a German artist from Mecklenburg who worked in England under the Italianate name of Francesco Cleyn and was employed by Charles I to design tapestries for the Mortlake factory. Posterity has almost totally forgotten Cleyn, a neglect which would have surprised him for he held himself in high esteem. 'Il famosissimo pittore, miracolo del secolo' appears as the legend to his self-portrait. But Dobson did Cleyn justice, for one of the few authentic records we have of him is his admission of indebtedness to the German master. Far better known was his subsequent employer and teacher the fashionable engraver Robert Peake for whom he appears to have done hack-work for some years.

The pleasant legend has it that Van Dyck, loitering one day among the print and picture dealers on Snow Hill, was struck by a painting exhibited for sale, inquired the artist's name and discovered Dobson in the proverbial garret. Whether the facts of their meeting were quite so fortuitous we may doubt. Dobson can hardly have lost touch altogether with the world of patronage in which his father had moved and the artist population of London in the 1630s was not so large but that the meeting of an evidently talented and interested young man with the all-conquering Van Dyck would be a matter of time. It was Van Dyck at all events who recommended him to the King, encouraged him in his work and presumably got him the entrée to the Royal collections which, with their notable examples of the late Venetian masters, were to have so strong an influence on his style.

King Charles, with one of his rare gracious phrases, called him the 'English Tintoret'. This is over-praise, but Dobson's dark, muscular style echoes far off the Italian master; less inventive, less powerful, more limited in colour and range, the English painter yet has an individuality which is unmistakably his own and which puts him outside the circle of Van Dyck's mere imitators. His fierce and virile touch was suited to the period in which he gathered his brief harvest, among the alarums of war. With what insight he fixed the features of this lost generation against the dark background, of these young soldiers who carried assurance on their brows and defeat in their hearts, of this whole doomed society which maintained to the last its interrupted culture, while the green college quadrangles were trampled bald by drilling feet, and Rupert's squadrons wheeled and formed in Christ Church meadows. Three winters and four summers he played his social and sociable part in the thronged city. He discussed archaeology with John Aubrey for whom he sketched the ruins of Osney; debated styles and techniques of painting with inquisitive Richard Symonds of the King's Lifeguard; caught his distinguished, hurried, military sitters as they came and went; until the hoarse gun on Magdalen Tower could make no more answer to the enemy guns drawing in from Marston, drawing in from Iffley, and the King's standard was hauled down from Christ Church and one day in June of the year 1646 the war, for Oxford, was ended.

Money had all the time been Dobson's difficulty. He is alleged in the troubled years at Oxford to have begun the practice of asking sitters for half the price in cash before he started. The precaution, which seems out of character with all we know of his feckless nature, did not help him much. Soon after the extinction of the King's cause he was in a London debtors' prison. An admirer bought him out, but his friends and his world were alike destroyed, and the ravages of consumption, unchecked by the unhealthy climate and too hectic life of Oxford, had gone too far. He died in the autumn of 1646, at about the same time as the Scots sold his most distinguished sitter to the English Parliament for two hundred thousand pounds.

STRAFFORD[1]

On May 12th, 1641, Thomas Wentworth, Earl of Strafford, was beheaded on Tower Hill. Although he inspired one of Macaulay's more terrific indictments and a play by Browning, he is not one of the best known of English statesmen. In the Whig tradition of history he stood out as the evil genius of Charles I, the proud, fearless, wicked man who was the energy and the brains of the King's unparliamentary rule. There was a time when even serious writers accepted unquestioning every private and public scandal connected with his name — how he violently ill-used his opponents, embezzled public funds and seduced the wife of one of his colleagues. Recent research has disproved the more outrageous slanders, and the change in the political climate which has caused a revaluation of Stuart policy has brought some belated recognition for his merits. It is now generally admitted that Strafford was an exceptionally gifted administrator and a statesman of high integrity of purpose.

A wealthy Yorkshire squire, he first attracted notice by refusing to pay the Forced Loan levied by the King in 1626, and in 1628 he led the House of Commons during the session which formulated the Petition of Right. At this point, however, his career took a sharp turn away from the Parliamentary party; he joined the Court side, became Lord President of the Council of the North and was given a seat on the Privy Council. In both these offices he at once made himself felt as a determined reformer, with the welfare of the common man and the intelligent ordering of public affairs at heart. From 1633 until 1639 he was Lord-Deputy of Ireland, where he pursued a sternly benevolent policy, controlled a subservient Parliament, checked the rapacity of the Anglo-Irish nobles and introduced some interesting social and

[1] *The Spectator*, May 12th, 1941.

economic legislation. Recalled to England in 1639 when the King's government was on the verge of collapse, he failed in the hopeless task of averting disaster. The royal army was defeated by the rebellious Scots and the King had no choice but to recall Parliament.

The Commons had never forgiven Strafford for his desertion of the Parliamentary side in 1628: he was the arch-traitor. Now, on the collapse of the King's personal rule, he made deliberate use of this fact, sacrificing himself to the animosity of the Commons in the hope of diverting popular ill-feeling from the King to himself. His political judgment may have been at fault in this, but at no time in his career does the individual man appear more noble than in this last attempt to save his master. The letter which he wrote to the King, urging him to appease the Commons by approving the Bill for his execution is at the same time one of the most extraordinary and one of the most moving documents in this language. 'To say that there has not been a strife in me,' he wrote, 'were to make me less man than, God Knoweth, my infirmities make me, and to call a destruction upon myself will find no easy consent from flesh and blood. To set Your Majesty's conscience at liberty, I do most humbly beseech Your Majesty ... to pass this Bill, and by this means to remove I cannot say this accursed, but I confess this unfortunate, thing forth of the way towards that blessed agreement which God, I trust, shall ever establish between you and your subjects.' That letter alone must confer on Strafford heroic stature.

So much for Strafford the man. But his fall stood for something more than the condemnation of a single man. Because of this larger issue, rather than because of intrinsic qualities, his fate deserves remembrance. His fall, and with it the end of King Charles's personal rule, marked the failure of a political experiment and the defeat of a principle. Although the personal rule of King Charles is now no longer believed to have been an uncompromising tyranny, and although the fair-minded admit that it was in many ways more beneficent to the common man than Parliamentary Government was to become for many generations, yet it was nevertheless a false start down a dangerous political path. It is therefore for the theory behind the King's actions and behind Strafford's that they must ultimately be judged, rather than for the intrinsic merits of those actions themselves. It is one of the paradoxes of history that the just men may sometimes be found defending the unjust cause while the self-interested may occasionally stumble into a right and noble course.

Writing of Strafford's fall, Archbishop Laud tried to explain it in personal terms: 'He served a mild and gracious Prince,' he wrote, 'who knew not how to be, or be made great.' Laud was wrong, for the fault was not in Charles, but in Charles's theory of Government and in Strafford's too practical contribution towards it. Strafford's administrative gift was his undoing, for like many good administrators he believed too much in authority. Much may be and must be sacrificed to efficiency, but one can sacrifice too much. That is the first maxim of democracy. To get rid of sloth and mismanagement Strafford was prepared to set the authority of the State beyond the reach of criticism. In the Ship-money case he described Hampden angrily as one of those whose nature 'leads them always to oppose all that authority ordains for them'. In the context one may sympathize, for with the seas infested with pirates and the navy in decay, Hampden's refusal to pay his contribution to the tax was, to say the least of it, inopportune. But in theory Strafford was wrong, for, whatever the circumstances, Hampden had a right to his opinion and Parliament should have been called. Once remove the citizen's right of criticism and no guarantee is left against the abuse of authority.

Was Strafford blind to this weakness in his case? Not altogether, for, like other authoritarians, he sought to surround his beliefs with a *mystique* — sure sign that he felt the need of a more profound justification than could be found in mere political practice.

Speaking in York, when he assumed his office of Lord President of the Council, he summed up his theory of the State. 'To the joint individual well-being of sovereignty and subjection', he said, 'do I here vow all my cares and diligences through the whole course of this my ministry . . . The authority of a King is the keystone which closeth up the arch of order and government, which contains each part in due relation to the whole . . . *Whatever he be that ravels forth into question the right of a King and of a people shall never be able to wrap them up again into the comeliness and order wherein he found them.*'

It was the fatal combination, administrative efficiency and the deification of the State. Did Strafford see to what excesses it might lead? Hardly, for he was all his life too busy a man to have time for remote speculation. He died in the conviction that the King's Government and his own must stand or fall by their practical results. A sincere, brave and able man, he lacked the vision to see that the State, like the human soul, cannot be saved by works alone.

FALKLAND [1]

PERSONALITIES which defy time are usually spectacular: a lively, rather than a placid, charm has survival value, and those figures whose immortality rests on *being*, not on *doing*, are on the whole rare — an occasional beauty, an occasional wit, an occasional 'character'. In politics they are fewer still, for in this field little save achievement commands immortality, unless it be a noble failure. Yet there are exceptions, and among the most notable perhaps that 'fine flame' of the Caroline age, Lord Falkland, who, on September 20th, 1643, rode headlong into a rain of musketry fire at the Battle of Newbury and was shot dead.

He was not the only distinguished Royalist to fall in the criss-cross of skirmishes among the square hedged fruit gardens and vegetable plots which ringed the market town of Newbury. It was a bad day for the peerage; the young lords Carnarvon and Sunderland were lost. Carnarvon is nothing now but one of those young men in dazzling satin from Van Dyck's family group in the double cube room at Wilton — he was Lord Pembroke's 'monstrous great ward' (meaning his fortune not his person) and had been married to his guardian's stodgy daughter. And Sunderland, who was not painted by Van Dyck, is less even than that; at twenty-three he had had no time to make his name, and, a victim of treacherous September weather, he met his death unromantically with a heavy cold in the head. 'Pray bless Popet for me', he had written to his wife on the previous day — 'Popet' was his daughter — and excused himself from further correspondence because 'I do nothing but sneeze'.

These two share a monument with Falkland on the field of Newbury; but he alone has a place in history. Why, one wonders, for he *did* very little. Can it be that he owes his immortality to

[1] *Time and Tide*, September 18th, 1943.

the chance of his friendship with Clarendon which got him so large a place in the *History of the Great Rebellion*? Or, can the 'incomparable young man', little as he achieved, stand on his own merits?

Small, unprepossessing, with a high, grating voice, Falkland's natural sweetness, his intelligence and good nature had the power to make anyone and everyone forget his extraordinary physical defects. Son of the Lord Deputy of Ireland, grandson and heir to the wealthy Lord Tanfield, educated in Dublin, he inherited at an early age an independent estate, married, to his father's apoplectic rage, the dowerless young woman whom he loved, and spent the blissful decade of the 1630s in keeping open house for the intelligentsia. In Parliament, however, he stood out as an enthusiastic defender of law in the State and liberty in the Church, yet sought — perhaps too late — to prevent the final breach with the King. Appointed, to his dismay, Secretary of State by Charles I, he followed his master loyally through the opening campaigns of the Civil War until his death at Newbury.

Not a great life, certainly; nor, on closer inquiry, a great intellect. Clarendon, with the partiality of affection, speaks of his 'prodigious parts of learning'; but they did not go beyond a good intelligence and an assiduous industry. He lacked originality. But he was analytically inclined, a careful and impartial critic with whom poets, philosophers and scholars could profitably discuss their work. At his house at Great Tew, conveniently near to Oxford, 'the most polite and accurate men of that university' were constantly to be found in fluent and informal session. So also were poets from the Court. There was something a little Russian about these unannounced week-enders, for their host himself frequently did not 'know of their coming or going, nor who were in the house, till he came to dinner, where still all met'. It sounds like something in Tchehov.

These unending house-parties, with their flowing talk and friendly arguments, were no preparation for the crisis between

King and Parliament so soon to arise in England. Yet if Falkland was unprepared and indeed unfitted for the harsher times to come, he was no escapist. Not for him to emulate the eccentric Lord Herbert of Cherbury, who refused the call to arms 'because I am newly entered into a course of physic', and remained pottering over his experiments at Montgomery. The underlying integrity of his character forbade such excuses; his sense of duty and his love of justice alike compelled him, the most tolerant of men, to take sides even in a quarrel he could not condone. Small wonder that, among the unreasonable clamours of war, 'dejection of spirit stole upon him', that he grew 'very sad, pale and exceedingly affected with the spleen', and at length sought the only way out by riding to certain death at Newbury.

Even in small things he had been oddly unfitted to the lawless exigencies of war. He abhorred spies and informers to such an extent that he would never use their services, which, for a Secretary of State in the seventeenth century, was to condemn himself to a perpetual working in the dark. Nor could he bring himself in any circumstances to the ungentlemanly act of opening other people's correspondence: intercepted treasonous letters accumulated on his desk with seals unbroken. Yet the impolite atmosphere of the camp—so different from that at Great Tew—had been brought home to him very early in the war when Prince Rupert, on the eve of Edgehill, busy with cavalry dispositions, had refused to receive him. 'In neglecting me, you neglect the King', protested Falkland. But that indeed was the order of the day; law and hierarchy were suspended, and the King himself had become an interfering civilian to be disregarded. *Inter arma silent leges*—and *reges* too, if the arms are to be successfully carried. It was because Charles would not put his army first that he lost his war — not to Parliament, but to Parliament's army.

All these things were beyond the experience and understanding of Falkland, nor was he to live to see the end. He belonged to that gentle preceding decade, that time of quietude and contemplation, of talking and thinking, of poetry, and music; the decade of George Herbert and Nicholas Ferrar, of Milton's *Comus* and Herrick's *Hesperides*, of Inigo Jones and Anthony Van Dyck, of William and Henry Lawes — in every sense except the political, the halcyon decade of the seventeenth century. His personality, fixed by Clarendon, has become almost symbolic of it, and his brief, unhappy experience in politics and war represents the attempt to fuse what could not be fused, to apply one set of values to another set of circumstances, the genius of peace to the demands of war.

REFLECTIONS ON THE GREAT CIVIL WAR

I. EDGEHILL, OCTOBER 23RD, 1642[1]

EDGEHILL rises sharply out of the rural uplands of Warwickshire, commanding, from the neo-gothic tower which absurdly crowns its height, one of the loveliest and most typical views in the country. Below the steep summit stretching away from the smooth lower slopes on which Prince Rupert's cavalry champed in line, lies, distance beyond distance, the green park-like expanse of Warwickshire irrelevantly scored with quickset hedges and narrow lanes, scattered with compact woodlands, starred here and there with those single magnificent trees which are so particular a feature of our countryside. I know of no part of England which the autumn visits with a more splendid glory, where the tenuous October sunlight touches more exquisitely the varying gold and green and brown of tree and hedgerow and field. It is a few miles only from Shakespeare's country, in the very heart of England.

The battle of Edgehill, was fought on an autumn afternoon, on October 23rd, 1642. It is not generally regarded as an important battle; text-books dismiss it as indecisive, and indecisive in a sense it was. For eighteen months before, the differences between King Charles I and his Parliament had slithered with disastrous rapidity from argument to defiance and from defiance to declared war. After a summer spent recruiting, the King had more or less decided to march on London, whence in the previous January he had fled, leaving Parliament in triumphant occupation. So here he was in the mild October weather riding disconsolately across the midlands at the head of an army. As usual, painfully racked

---

[1] *Time and Tide*, August 22nd and October 24th, 1942.

between two alternatives, he contemplated sometimes the forcible occupation of the capital and the silencing of the Commons, and at others a compromise settlement. At Edgehill he found himself suddenly faced with the alternative in all its shocking nakedness. Here was, from the military point of view, the big opportunity. Prince Rupert, his nephew, who had turned out quite by chance to be a born general, had outflanked the Parliamentary army under Essex and installed the King's troops on the summit of Edgehill in a position to deliver a shattering blow. The Parliamentary army, at that time even more amateurish than the King's, lay sprawled in the uneven country below; if it could be put out of action the road to London would be comparatively clear. The Civil War would be over by Christmas.

But Rupert and the few other professional soldiers on either side had failed to understand the extraordinary nature of the conflict in which they found themselves engaged. At that time only a minority on either side wanted to deliver a smashing blow at anyone. The greater number were still uncertain whether they wanted to fight at all, and a considerable proportion had not even made up their minds conclusively as to which side they were on. The King's standard bearer, Sir Edmund Verney, was in a typical state of anxiety and doubt: his eldest son was sitting in Parliament at Westminster. He was not the only one whose family had been torn in pieces by the war, for it was a period at which men's consciences were highly individual and uncomfortably active.

The King had reproduced the uncertainty in his own mind by dividing the command of his troops. Rupert, theoretically Lieutenant-General of the Horse, was in active command only on the right wing. The left was under Wilmot, a pleasant, indolent young man with a smattering of military experience and a fairly evident desire not to annoy Parliament too much, lest Parliament should win. The commandership in chief, so far as there was one at all, was supposed to belong to an elderly soldier of fortune,

Patrick Ruthven, who, in the days before he became stone deaf, had been quartermaster-general to Gustavus Adolphus.

The battle therefore lacked any coherent plan. Rupert's initial charge drove the Parliamentary left wing off the field, but there was considerable delay in re-forming his newly-recruited and untrained troops, and meanwhile the infantry in the centre, commanded with equal courage and almost equal inefficiency on both sides, were locked in a life and death struggle. Rupert's return relieved the situation, but although a few of the Royalist officers argued that a new attack on the exhausted and half-scattered enemy would be decisive, the majority felt that there had been enough fighting for one day. The occasion once lost never recurred. The battle of Edgehill was thus not so indecisive as it appeared, for never again was the King to have so evident an opportunity of ending the war at a stroke.

Edgehill was the first important engagement in a struggle which was to last intermittently for ten years, and was to fire and crystallize those rival theories of government which had been locked in bloodless conflict for the last quarter of a century. The ideas involved were fundamentally simple: absolutism against representative government. Was Parliament to develop as the legislative body of the kingdom, or was it to be transformed into a mere advisory committee with no coercive power? The issue has been confused by those writers who have recently pointed out that King Charles was on the whole an enlightened and benevolent ruler (making allowance for the occasional ear-croppings of his Court of Star Chamber), while Parliament, far from representing the people, was a fairly close oligarchy of the landed and monied class. The exercise of the representative principle in 1642 meant the representation of propertied men by a number of their own magnates and a hand-picked selection of their younger sons.

The Civil War was certainly no struggle of the people against the Crown; it was in a different tradition from the national and proletarian revolts of the nineteenth and twentieth centuries. Yet the principles involved are fundamental to government, as fundamental now as then. The struggle may not have been in the modern sense 'democratic', yet had it not happened or had it ended differently, the history of democracy in Europe, and far beyond Europe, would have been changed. For this war saved the principle of representative government, and saved it in that very country whose language and whose people were to be one of the great vitalizing forces of the New World. It was at this period, the period when men in England thought it worth while to fight for the representative principle, that the New England colonies were being founded, by the fathers and sons and brothers of the men fighting in England.

Had King Charles won the war in that first campaign would the principle have survived? It is dangerous to speculate on might-have-beens, yet the survival of effective representative government after a Royalist victory would have been improbable, and if the principle had gone under in England, as it did in so many other European countries at about this time, what might not have happened on the far side of the Atlantic? It is instructive to compare the history of the Spanish and the French Empires in America with that of the English colonies. These became a nation through rightly interpreting the political principles which the mother country had established a century earlier, and which, owing to the drag of certain reactionary forces, she had illogically failed to extend to her children.

Much then may have depended on this unfinished and inde-cisive battle. At the close of the day when the Royalist com-manders were discussing the possibility of a renewed attack, the casual Henry Wilmot argued that quite enough had been done: and it was time to pause and 'enjoy the fruits thereof'. In a sense of which Henry Wilmot never dreamed, men unborn and lands unknown were to enjoy the fruits thereof.

In our rather shamefaced attempts to advertise our country to the foreigner, we make too little of the Civil War. It happened of course a very long time ago — though not so long ago as Joan of Arc or William the Silent, who are, or were, emphatically honoured in their own countries; and not nearly so long ago as the proto-German Arminius. It happened, perhaps unfortunately, at a period whose fashions in dress lend themselves to romantic treatment, so that in the popular mind this Cavalier-and-Roundhead business has degenerated into a clashing-sword accompaniment to many a stirring love drama. It even went abroad in this form and in the nineteenth century reached the Italian operatic stage in *I Puritani*. Measures of counter-action do not seem to have been strong enough. It is true that English historians have treated the conflict with dignity and at length and that the text-books have built it firmly and, on the whole, correctly into the fabric of constitutional development. But there, as far as the general public are concerned, it remains — fossilized, an antique.

Yet its very antiquity is all the more cause for admiration. Is it not worthy of comment that the English contrived to fight so remarkably *adult* a war at a time when no other people in Europe seem to have been, politically, more than adolescent? Compare this struggle with the pointless horror of Germany's coeval Thirty Years War, with the *mesquineries* of the Fronde, with the spasmodic, unconstructive separatist outbursts in contemporary Spain and Italy. The English Civil War is set apart from these by the more adult consciousness of the participants. Men that 'made some conscience of what they did', Cromwell said; but the description fitted many of the Royalist soldiers, no less. Chillingworth wittily deplored the fact that all the scribes and pharisees were on one side, all the publicans and sinners on the other; but it was a half truth only, for pharisees and sinners there will always be in all conflicts. What distinguishes the English Civil War is the astonishing prevalence of plain sincerity on both sides. Moreover, the combatants never wholly lost sight of the purpose of the war; they were fighting for the better governance of England, and they never forgot that they must learn to live in peace hereafter with the men who were ranged against them. It would be absurd to pretend that there were no savage incidents, no persecution of the defeated, no acts of vengeance. There were all these. But they never became ends in themselves, never submerged the higher purpose of both parties.

Any detailed study of the combatants, any inquiry into their private lives, reveals the absurdity of those theories which explain the Civil War as a blockish alignment of class or interest. Men followed their beliefs with an independent fidelity; no class, no group, no family that was not split along the line of personal conviction. The 'money-power' in which some recent writers have tried to mask the parliamentarian party simply did not exist as a united political unit. Its representatives are to be found both at the King's right-hand and tub-thumping with the Levellers. There were of course the usual number of time-servers, scoundrels, profiteers, yes-men and fools on both sides. Nor were the motives of any man or any group above suspicion. Self-interest was a powerful motive force. When has it not been? It was as much to the King's interest to maintain his own power as it was to that of the English gentry in Parliament to stand out for theirs; naturally. Yet the Civil War was not a selfish struggle for supremacy. Government not *of*, but *for*, the people was the ultimate end of the best men in both parties. They had, deeply ingrained, a saving sense of moral responsibility.

Ten years of fighting and nearly twenty years of unrest may seem a high price to have paid for the Restoration of King Charles II and a working compromise the virtues of which became only gradually apparent. War is always an uneconomic price to pay: although it may be the only one. Yet whatever its outcome the Civil War broadcast among the people theories, experiments, ideas and suggestions, some of which were to germinate for a later harvest. It produced in *The Agreement of the People* a document which is the first modern charter of democracy — and an admirable one it is.

Those who first challenged the King's right to govern without Parliament, those who first raised the representative against the absolutist principle, may have conceived of Parliament as a body of propertied men chosen by propertied men. But they had set a train of action moving which they could not themselves stop, and they were to find among their own number before the end of the war those who saw the true bearing of the principle. 'I think', said Thomas Rainborough, colonel of artillery and Member of Parliament for Droitwich, 'I think that the meanest He that is in England hath a life to live as well as the greatest He: and therefore, truly sir, I think it clear that every man that is to live under a government ought, first, by his own consent to put himself under that Government.' He meant manhood suffrage and was not alone in meaning it.

For the time being the men of property carried the day, though perhaps only because Thomas Rainborough was killed in a scuffle at Doncaster. It was to need another two and a half centuries until the 'meanest He that is in England' (let alone the meanest She) got a voice in the Government. But the foundation had been laid: the words had been spoken.

II. JOHN HAMPDEN[1]

'We had catched each others' locks, and sheathed our swords in each others' bowels, had not the sagacity and great calmness of Mr. Hampden, by a short speech, prevented it.' The scene in the House of Commons thus recorded by a sitting member happened three hundred years ago when the locks of M.P.s were of a length to be 'catched' by angry opponents, though sheathing swords in each other's bowels was not, even then, an English custom. Otherwise Mr. Hampden's short speech would not so easily have prevented it. A few months later, it is true, civil war

[1] *Time and Tide*, June 26th, 1943.

between King and Parliament had broken out and Englishmen were slaughtering each other — but at least they were doing it *al fresco*, not among the benches of the House of Commons.

Hampden's typical intervention to still the rising passions of his fellow members came into my mind when I recollected that on June 24th of this year three full centuries had passed since 'John Hampden, the patriot' (as old histories used to call him) died at Thame of the wound he had received six days before during the skirmish on Chalgrove Field. Much water has flowed under the bridge since then; time has swept this and that away, submerged a great number of reputations and cast up others upon its banks as swollen, unrecognizable corpses. Only a few remain, and Hampden's, if a little battered, is still among them.

'With great courage, and consummate abilities, he began a noble opposition to an arbitrary court, in defence of the liberties of his country; supported them in Parliament, and died for them in the Field': thus a lapidary tribute chiselled midway between his time and ours, but after the poet Gray had aptly turned him into a household word with his 'village Hampden that with dauntless breast the little tyrant of his fields withstood'. In his own time opinions were divided. 'A man of that prudence, judgment, temper, valour and integrity, that he hath left few his like behind him', wrote his Parliamentary obituarist; but the Royalist Clarendon attributed to him 'a head to contrive, and a tongue to persuade, and a hand to execute, any mischief'; and the authoritarian Strafford said sourly that he was one of those 'whose nature leads them always to oppose all that authority ordains for them'.

That is the crux of the matter, at least as far as we are concerned, for we have come again to that recurrent political cross-road which John Hampden and his contemporaries knew. We have changed our patter and brought our methods up to date, but the political labyrinth is the same, seeming larger perhaps and more crowded, but with the same dead-ends and by-roads. The problem of 1643 is the problem of to-day, only more vast, complex and insoluble; you cannot dispense with authority, but you must not let authority dispense with you. 'Now, *here*' — as the Red Queen said — 'it takes all the running *you* can do, to keep in the same place.'

Not that we are in every respect in the same place as John Hampden. Evidently not. His world was smaller and simpler than ours, and his problem by that much the more straightforward. The national issue could be kept apart from the international as it cannot be to-day, and Englishmen in his time had few responsibilities outside England. But no country can escape its past, least of all a country like our own with a political tradition exceptionally self-consistent. Hampden and Hampden's problem belong to us for good, and the division from us in time is no division from us in understanding. Much of our cultural and historic heritage is the same: we share with him for instance Queen Elizabeth, Shakespeare and Magna Carta, though we have got the Industrial Revolution, Enclosure and the British Empire as well. The average living Englishman has more in common with John Hampden — dead three hundred years — than he has with Gandhi or with Stalin.

When Hampden refused to pay Ship-money solely because the King had imposed the tax without consulting Parliament, his conduct was *comprehensible* to the generality of his compatriots, whether they approved it or not. But it amazed the Venetian envoy: 'They stick to their laws', he wrote home, 'and allow legal proceedings to be taken, solely to make it known that the laws are violated, and that they are compelled to pay by force.' Hampden was no demagogue and no idealist; he believed that the rights of man would look after themselves if the rights of Parliament were secure. He stood out — as a German historian has expressed it in a slightly puzzled way — 'not for a shining ideal, but for a statutory right' — the statutory right of Parliament to control taxation. In outline the story is not heroic. A very rich man refused to pay 20s. towards the expenses of the navy, which

was in the direst need, because the King had not formally sub-
mitted his plan to Parliament. No martyr's stake was involved,
no concentration camp, merely expensive legal proceedings and
possible detention at the King's pleasure, which — for a wealthy
man in the seventeenth century — did not mean prison in our
sense of the word at all.

Why did he do it? The wealthy Parliamentarian leaders have
been much mocked of late. They acted, we are told, from self-
interest, to defend their influence as a class. The 'money-power'
feared that the Crown would usurp its own particular right of
exploiting the people. Talk of ancient English liberties was, it is
said, mere eye-wash. Well, there is something in that too,
though I think it would have distressed and astonished Hampden.
But it is not in the nature of men to act ideally, and we know
to-day that the nearest we can, any of us, get to sincerity is
perhaps a genuine self-deception.

The significance of an act is not to be measured by its heroism
or even by its sincerity. When Hampden refused to pay Ship-
money he put up his hand like a policeman at the most dangerous
cross-road in our history and firmly diverted the traffic. And
there is no doubt whatever which way the traffic was going. A
period of disorder and transition, the preceding century had
caused all over Europe a terrifying increase in authority. The
practice of representative government, quietly developing
through the middle ages, had broken down under the joint
pressure of Renaissance and Reformation. Machiavelli had
codified *Realpolitik* and Divine Right had endowed despotism
with a *mystique*. Dictatorship alone seemed capable of solving the
problem of social order.

There was much to be said for it, as there always is. How easy
it would be if the enemy held no trump cards! But the authoritarians have always held a good hand: they offer benefits dis-
mayingly real and quickly to be had — order, peace, security,
national greatness. You have only to open your mouth and shut

your eyes and the benevolent despot will pop a sugar plum between your lips. For nine people out of ten this is gag enough, and for the tenth there are other methods. So the monarchies grow absolute, and the dictators rise, and there follows, at best, lethargy and corruption, at worst, gangsterdom and international war.

III. GOVERNMENT BY CONSENT[1]

Ten days after the anniversary of Hampden's death the historical calendar records an anniversary which does not need the special circumstance of a tercentenary to secure its due observance — Independence Day.

The juxtaposition is a happy one, for we cannot too often recall our common heritage with the people of the United States. Doctrines of government, established during the English conflict of the seventeenth century, were faithfully preserved across the Atlantic, and the American colonists seceded for that very principle of government by consent — or, in detail, of no taxation without representation — for which Hampden had stood, and which indeed without his timely intervention might have perished among the Anglo-Saxon people as it did elsewhere.

It is very old indeed, this principle of no taxation without representation, very old, very simple and very important. Unfortunately also, it is a principle which can easily be ridiculed and misinterpreted, for it is not precisely a beautiful or an uplifting idea. Practical and business-like, it has remained — and will remain, as long as money is the sinews of the State — the most essential of the political rights of man, but it has not, baldly stated, power to inflame the heart. It was claimed before this war that nobody could be expected to go out and fight for a mere 'standard of living', nor have men perished in the field or on the scaffold for the unadorned principle of no taxation without representation. They have died for it wholeheartedly when it

[1] *Time and Tide*, July 3rd, 1943.

has been called the Will of God or the Rights of Man. We cannot do without these expansions and adornments, these slight disguises.

Later, of course, retribution falls on the coiners of fine phrases, when some of their descendants, prying into cause and effect, discover (with rather ingenuous surprise) that our ancestors were no better than ourselves, and that their noble ideals concealed motives which were sometimes personally and almost always politically self-interested. With unconcealed *Schadenfreude*, these debunkers tumble the economic skeleton out of the cupboard and warn us against being deceived by words alone.

Undoubtedly it was a blindness in our forefathers — though one from which they derived nothing but strength — that they underestimated or concealed their more selfish motives. But their principles, now seen to be so heavily involved with loss and gain, do not thereby become of less importance to the welfare and even the freedom of mankind. No one with any real knowledge of political development in Western Europe can doubt that the general tendency towards absolutism, which set in about the time of the Renaissance was, in spite of any incidental benefits, a bad and a dangerous thing. No amount of special pleading for this dynasty or that monarch, no revelations about Hampden's investments, can radically alter this fact. No group, no Party has ever acted with motives entirely pure, and it is well to remember that all of us are, in the words of Belloc, 'pretty nearly all day long doing something rather wrong'. This goes for Left and Right, Whig and Tory, Communist, Liberal and Fascist, and is not — as is generally believed — a monopoly of the 'other side'.

With these limitations, we may accept the *bona fides* of the seventeenth-century conflict and respect the virtues and the theories of our ancestors with no more reserve than did their American descendants in 1776. The consanguinity between the champions of Parliamentary Government in England and the founders of American democracy is exceptionally clear. There are, of course, changes of fashion and outlook to be reckoned with. Morality, in 1776, has nature for its framework and not religion; we feel the physiocrats behind the *Declaration of Independence* as we feel the sectarians behind so many of the political utterances of the English Civil War; Divine Providence has replaced that menacing individual 'the Lord', and 'the laws of nature and of nature's God' the specific mandates of Holy Writ. The *Declaration of Independence* is a wider and more spacious Document belonging to a more spacious epoch. But the spirit of the Parliamentarian conflict is there: the same emphasis on legal as well as on moral justification, the same insistence on the reconstitution of accepted, rather than the establishment of new, rights. The salient points of the Parliamentarian case re-emerge clause by clause — the appointment of judges, the control of armed forces, the prevention of dictatorial interference with the legislature, the strengthening of the representative assembly, and the root principle of no taxation without representation.

The Anglo-Saxon contribution to the political evolution of mankind is thus exceptionally consistent and practical. It is also of immeasurable value. But it is not the only solution of the problem of government; it is a solution within a particular framework and by a particular group of peoples. Writing in the middle of the nineteenth century, Bancroft, the historian of the United States, could speak without further definition of the 'immutable principles of morals', of the 'unchangeableness of freedom, virtue and right'. We cannot speak so to-day; even our imperfect knowledge of the remote and complex civilizations which have lived, and which still live, on the surface of the globe, even the primitive researches of anthropologists and psychologists reveal variations on the theme of morality and government which reduce or reverse the authenticity of principles once thought of as absolute. 'The heart of Jefferson in writing the Declaration, and of congress adopting it', says Bancroft, 'beat for all humanity.' For the negro slaves? for the Russians? for the Chinese . . .? 'All humanity' is an elastic phrase and has been used to cover as vast a number of races and peoples as a single mind can imagine, or, with equal sincerity, to indicate a section of the educated classes.

Between Hampden and Jefferson, the human landscape had opened out. Between Jefferson and ourselves, it has grown almost too gigantic for the single brain to master its variety. Nevertheless, abused or not, 'humanity' is an ennobling concept; to think of 'humanity' and to think for 'humanity', however narrowly the bounds are drawn, is an achievement for the limited mind of the individual man, the greatest achievement which civilization has to its credit and the object, in the end, of all civilization.

WILLIAM PENN[1]

I SHALL not easily forget the impact of my first encounter with William Penn. It happened in the pages of Besse's *Sufferings of the Quakers* which I was turning over in search of material on Non-conformity in the early days of Charles II. Taken unadulterated, Besse is gloomy reading, in spite of the lucid faith which shines from every page. Browbeaten, bullied, insulted, the Quakers struggled on, with the law closing in remorselessly against them. More than four thousand were in prison by 1662. The creed of non-violence always exasperates the violent; local persecution pursued them, justices of the peace delighted to make them the butts of coarse merriment, the Lord Mayor of London particularly disliked them. Patient, obstinate, equable and full of apt quotations from the Scriptures, the Quakers were not put out of countenance. They were simply shouted down.

Shouted down, evicted, expelled, carted off to prison . . . the Quakers' story seemed symbolic of the eternal helplessness of the innocent and the good in the struggle not with evil (for there the fight is open and equal) but with stupidity and ill-nature in high places. What could they do, these saintly shoemakers and country folk? What can they ever do?

At this moment in my reading and my thoughts appeared the marginal entry *Comitment of W. Penn*, and the youthful son of a choleric Admiral (who had recently thrown him out of his house) strode into the picture and turned the tables on authority.

The reason? He spoke the same language. Trained in the law, he challenged them with retorts not from the Gospels but from their own law books until the maddened Recorder of London wished aloud for the powers of the Spanish Inquisition to quell him. To prevent disorder in the court he had him shut up out of

[1] *Time and Tide*, October 21st, 1944.

sight in the baledock whose wooden walls were higher than the prisoner's head. Penn could still hear what was going on and, detecting a further irregularity, hoisted himself into view with gymnastic skill and loudly cited Coke's Second Institute. The jury acquitted him. The Recorder bade them think again. They still acquitted him. The Recorder fined them forty marks each. Penn's voice was instantly upraised. 'Take him away', shrieked the Recorder. 'I can never urge the fundamental laws of England', said Penn, 'but you cry: "Take him away".'

In the outcome the jurors brought and won an action against the Recorder; Lord Chief Justice Vaughan uttered his celebrated vindication of the freedom of juries and an important point was scored in constitutional law.

Triumph. But was it quite the triumph the Quakers wanted? Penn had vindicated the fundamental laws, not of God, but of England. The issue has subtly changed from faith to politics.

This is by no means to belittle William Penn; great courage and great faith are needed wilfully to compromise a hopeful career, to embrace a persecuted sect, to endure long imprisonment with equanimity. Yet the dazzling Inner Light of a George Fox or a James Naylor seems reduced in William Penn to the pleasant glow of a domestic lamp. We are sometimes called on to-day to admire Penn for his noble failures, his visions of universal peace and brotherly love; this too lofty view clashes inevitably with the Penn of history, the 'talking, vain man' whom Bishop Burnet knew, with the 'tedious, luscious way' he imagined to be persuasive. Impossible not to feel, watching this other Penn, that the bold perceptions of the young Quaker had later become embedded in layers of self-satisfied benevolence. Self-satisfaction went before disaster. His dabbling in politics was unsuccessful and some of the mud thrown at him for playing the courtier to James II stuck; estrangement from Friends followed, strife in Pennsylvania, debts, accusations, distrust. The overburdened mind found release in a return to childhood until a benign old gentleman vacantly ambling after butterflies was all that remained of William Penn.

His reputation had already declined when he wrote that little work *The Fruits of Solitude*, the 'sweet, dignified and wholesome book' in which R. L. Stevenson found 'so much honest, kind wisdom'. That it has certainly. In one incomparable phrase only does this manual of courageous common sense light up suddenly with the flame of an eternal truth — 'They that love beyond the World cannot be separated by it'. But for the rest, the honest, kind wisdom remains earthbound.

More than any other single influence Penn seems to have given to the Friends their reputation and their bent for practical Christianity, their orientation, as it were, away from mysticism to prison reform. (Penn's own views on prisons were astonishingly in advance of his time.) These are great things, but they are not the greatest, and the abiding strength of the Friends derives from a source nobler than utilitarian goodness.

Yet the first step towards the civilized State — the State whose object is the Good Life — must be the concrete admission of the dignity of the human soul. Without this the spiritual capacities of man are for ever frustrated. Penn abhorred, in his own words, 'Obedience upon Authority, without Conviction'. The human mind must be free to choose.

When it came to conflict with authority, his feet were as firmly on the ground as those of any lawyer in England. He saw to it that Magna Carta was printed in Philadelphia, thus bringing (along with Quaker doctrine) the fundamental laws of England to the New World. So, too, in England itself, he had defended God's word through the words of Sir Edward Coke.

We cannot, I think, put him among the greatest, not with those who, like Faithful, go 'with Sound of Trumpet, the nearest way to the Celestial Gate'. But without him and his kind, never a Faithful of this world but will be burnt at the stake in Vanity Fair.

THE CONVERSION OF MALTA[1]

Two Englishwomen, middle-aged and soberly clad, each with a large, corded trunk, embarked on a Dutch ship at Leghorn early in the year 1659. They booked their passage with the Captain as far as Alexandria, where, they told him, it was their mission 'to preach the Gospel of Christ to the inhabitants'. Whatever he thought of their prospects, he made no comment.

They were West Country women of the sober, fearless, respectable middle-class; their names — already known to several irate magistrates of England — were Katherine Evans and Sarah Chevers. For some years now, leaving home and kindred, they had travelled preaching together, facing the stocks, the whipping-post and furious objurgations from the Bench with that limitless brave innocence which was the characteristic of their faith. They were of the Society of Friends.

They had been storm tossed and sea-sick on the long journey from London to Leghorn, and although they looked undismayed on the swarthy people, and the evidences of idolatry in churches with more towers, turrets and bells even than the 'steeple-houses' of England, they had evidently been glad to fall in with kindly merchants of their own faith at Leghorn. Now they were setting out for un-known territory, leaving the strange coast of Italy, with its foreign architecture and unfamiliar vegetation, for lands even more unimaginable. The honest timbers of their Dutch vessel were the last link between them and the comprehensible, Protestant north. Not that, moving trance-like at the guidance of the Lord, they would have paused to admit such feelings. They were, among Papists or Infidels, in Italy or Africa, always in the hands of God.

Women of character and courage, versed in the Scriptures and in little else, Katherine had the readier and the sharper tongue,

[1] *Windmill*, June 1946.

Sarah had the louder voice for preaching and the greater persistence in what she undertook. Both, like many Englishwomen before and since, were indifferent to ridicule. They would do as they thought right, whether they should be mocked by rude boys or burnt alive.

Not far out from Leghorn, their ship changed course, to have the companionship of another vessel, in the pirate-infested seas, as far as Malta. When the Captain informed his English passengers of the new plan, they knew at once, by revelation, how fateful Malta would be to them and Katherine was moved of the Lord to cry out: 'Oh we have a dreadful cup to drink at that place!'

Their first sight of the island confirmed both their faith and their fears. Standing on the deck, they saw with wonder the crowded, scrambling city, its walls and windows alive with a dark-faced, strange humanity. Unused to Mediterranean crowds they took this for a phenomenon peculiar to the day of their arrival and immediately went to their cabin to pray. It had become clear to them that Alexandria was not to be. Malta – the island on which Saint Paul had been shipwrecked – was their appointed place.

While they were below, the English Consul came on board to see the Captain. He left for the English ladies an invitation to his house, possibly in the hope of restraining whatever activities they had planned. The island, which was ruled over by the Grand Master of the Knights of St. John of Jerusalem, was a stronghold of the Church militant and the Inquisition was active.

Neither Knights nor Inquisition daunted Katherine and Sarah. On the following day, each carrying a bundle of tracts, they set off for the Consul's house. Over light refreshments he introduced them to two or three Jesuits. He made no secret of the fact that his sympathy was with the government and official religion of Malta – he could hardly otherwise have maintained himself as consul – but he evidently hoped to carry off the situation by treating the newcomers as diverting eccentrics. The sharp eyes of Katherine and Sarah saw through him at once, though they accepted his invitation to visit his sister, a nun, on the following day. In the nuns' parlour their simple manners and the novelty of their conduct made a pleasant break in the dull routine of convent life, but there was temporary embarrassment when, on being shown over the buildings and chapel, they not only refused to bow to the altar but profited by the occasion to deliver a short lecture on the evils of idolatry.

Meanwhile their ship had sailed, and since they insisted on staying, trunks, tracts, and all, the consul — by this time acutely anxious — thought best to continue his hospitality, if only to supervise their conduct. The Inquisition was not an institution to be lightly challenged and he could not have Katherine and Sarah jeopardizing the good repute of the English colony. His plan had some effect for, in spite of his guests' inclination to rise up and prophesy in and out of season, more especially at open windows, fifteen weeks went by before the Inquisition made its deadly pounce. When it did he was not sorry to lose them; he had given them fair and repeated warning.

The Maltese Inquisition, which was the Roman, not the Spanish, Inquisition was strict in suppressing heresies, but had not the gruesome and highly regulated methods of Spain. The two women seem to have been confined in the ordinary prison, their examination and conversion being entrusted almost wholly to the English friars in the place. The small English colony, mostly converts, took the liveliest interest in them; the more obstinate did Katherine and Sarah become, the more did it grow to a point of honour with their compatriots to bring them back to the Mother Church. It was almost as if their conversion were to be a symbol of the return of the whole erring motherland.

Katherine and Sarah found themselves at first shut into a small inner room with 'two little holes in it for light and air'. They were much tormented 'with flies called muskatoes', nor were these the worst they had to suffer; they had no means of washing, no fresh air, their hair began to drop out, their skins grew rough as 'sheep's leather', and they had to lie down and breathe through the door chink from time to time so as not to be stifled.

In this horrible den they were constantly visited by the friars, and here, day after day, feverish, unwashed and unafraid they defied their interlocutors, triumphantly capping every quotation from Holy Writ and scornfully dismissing arguments from other sources. Their Bibles were soon taken away: vain precaution, they knew them by heart. More than usually exasperated by Sarah's pat, decisive answers one friar declared 'he saw an evil spirit in her face'. With unexpected personal vanity, she was indignant; she thought he meant the ravages of the 'muskatoes' on her complexion.

Katherine, meanwhile, was comforted by a vision in the night and soon after, extracting pen, ink and paper from her precious trunk, indited a letter to the chief Inquisitor. 'To the Lord Inquisitor (so-called)', she headed it, and went on: 'Men's persons I cannot admire; they that do admire and respect any Man's person, do it because of advantage.' After this preamble she called him to order in the name of the Lord. Pen and ink were shortly after removed from her.

The prohibition seems to have been relaxed or evaded later, for both women wrote letters home and Katherine composed a continuous stream of reflections, prayers and hymns. Captivity and daily arguments were not soothing to her soul and the thought of the Day of Judgment gave her grim comfort:

> Then some shall howl and some shall mourn
> The rest shall wish they'd ne'er been born
> For Pain and Torment Day and Night,
> Because they have despis'd the Light —

Yet to consign all Malta and the friars to perdition was not primarily her intention; she would gladly have saved them. At every possible opening in the examinations both she and Sarah reversed the order of proceedings and began to convert their converters.

Not for some months did their captors take the obvious step of separating them. Perhaps they had no other cell vacant before, since the new cell found for Sarah was not, from their point of view, a happy choice. It gave on an alley way leading from a Court of Justice to a Church. Never a procession went by but she would be at her window loudly — and in English — exhorting the worshippers to repent. Soon after a fleet of twenty sail assembled off Malta to go against the Turks and the city was full of soldiers and sailors, both French and Italian. 'Go not forth to murder, nor to kill one another', cried Sarah from her window to the troops pouring into the Church to pray for victory. It was no use; the fleet sailed, the Turks were defeated and to Sarah's grief 'there was great triumphing and glorying in Blood'.

The determination of the English friars to make converts, not martyrs, of the Quaker women, must have been the chief factor in preserving their lives. But in the early days of their imprisonment they were in real danger and constantly threatened with torture and burning. Katherine and Sarah, both doubtless well primed from childhood with atrocity stories of the Inquisition, never doubted the validity of the threats. And indeed it must remain something of a mystery why none of them was carried out; neither in its course nor in its conclusion was the case a typical one.

Cut off from all intercourse with people of their own language (except the friars), locked up without hope of release, expecting daily their final martyrdom and trembling with fear every time a loud Mediterranean brawl occurred within earshot — which was often — the two women, alone or together, in sickness or in health remained unshaken. They held fast not only to their religious tenets but to all the other peculiar rulings of their faith. They would take no oath, they would borrow no money, they would bow to no authority; they would not even say in advance when or what they would eat, lest the Lord should command them otherwise at the last minute. They were proof against threats and against temptation; when attempts at conversion took on a different form and they were coaxed with tales of how much they would be cherished by the whole English colony, and indeed all Malta, if they gave in, they were unmoved. The Inquisitor, hearing that Katherine was by this time really ill, sent her a present of two plump fowls. She refused them saying firmly that she would live only of her own, and Sarah, whom they next tried to trick into cooking them behind Katherine's back, was equally emphatic.

Both women had so far paid all their expenses punctually, but at the end of one year and seven weeks their stock of money was exhausted. From this time onwards, the Inquisition having lost all but a theoretical interest in them, they were allowed to go among the other prisoners, and soon found means both to pay their way and to introduce an air of middle-class respectability into the gaol, by knitting stockings and neatly darning clothes for their companions. When not preaching they were gentle, kindly and efficient creatures and seem to have been liked, although they provoked derision when, from time to time they dishevelled their hair, cast dust on their heads and did loud penance for the sins of Malta. Greater misgivings were expressed when they washed the dust out of their hair by dipping their heads into buckets of cold water. But, as Katherine triumphantly observed, vindicating English habits of personal cleanliness, 'they caught no cold, nor had so much as the snuff in their Noses'.

Spasmodic efforts were by this time being made for their release. A new English Consul, more sympathetic than the last, assisted by the English Captain of a passing vessel, prevailed so far with the authorities that Katherine and Sarah could have sailed back to England at once if they would have consented merely to kiss the crucifix. (This at least was what they understood the condition to be.) Valiant and exasperating women, they utterly refused. Thinking that 'idolatry' was their chief trouble the patient Consul tried again, and this time procured their release on condition that some reputable citizen would go bail for their staying away from Malta. Neither Katherine nor Sarah would hear of it: it made them debtors to a third party. Besides the Lord had made his will known to Katherine and it was not yet his will that they should leave.

The new Consul gave it up. His embarrassment was increased by the arrival, soon after, of a Quaker minister named Daniel Baker whom the Turks had expelled from Smyrna. No sooner was he landed, than he wrote to the prisoners, 'Dear Lambs, Peace be unto you', with several pages more of spiritual consolation. For the rest he contrived to talk to them through the prison grating and to utter a certain number of home truths about the spiritual darkness of Malta before the harassed Consul hustled him on board a ship for England. He was not a popular passenger, for at Gibraltar, on Holy Thursday, he slipped ashore, marched into a local church, strode up the aisle and after derisively watching the priest for some minutes, turned his back on the altar, rent his garments, sprinkled a handful of dust on his head and in resonant biblical English called on the worshippers to repent. They must have taken him for more of a lunatic than a heretic, for no one touched him, though the Captain of the ship left Gibraltar in a hurry and, as Baker wonderingly noticed, 'spake bitter Things against him'.

By this time, however, George Fox himself was anxious that something should be done for the prisoners at Malta, and George Fox had a powerful streak of common sense. Evidently the only way in which the two women could be unconditionally released was by the direct intervention, not merely of a higher but of the highest authority. Someone must approach the Pope.

A possible intermediary, the London Quakers suggested, was the King's cousin, 'Lord d'Aubenay'. This gentleman, whose name was Ludovic Stuart, was a cadet of the royal family, and had been brought up largely in France, where he had taken orders and become a canon of Notre-Dame. In spite of his priestly office he had quietly assumed the title of his elder brother, George Lord d'Aubigny, when the latter was killed fighting on the King's side at Edgehill. Since George left a voluble widow and a son, the family thought poorly of Ludovic's conduct, but the subsequent accession of the real Lord d'Aubigny to the Dukedom of Richmond had, so to speak, evened out the honours.

Ludovic Stuart, whatever his greed for worldly titles, had gracious manners and a not unkindly heart. The Quakers found him 'a well-temper'd Man . . . notwithstanding he was a Priest in Orders belonging to the Romish Church'. Besides being 'well-temper'd' he had through his royal connections the necessary personal influence. With surprisingly little delay, in July 1662, the Vatican gave orders for the unconditional release of the two prisoners at Malta.

Even so Katherine and Sarah distinguished clearly between the will of Christ's Vicar ('so-called') and the will of Christ. There was a moment's painful anxiety for the English Consul while they awaited the Inner Light. It came: they might leave their prison. They packed their deplenished trunks, took care to tip their gaolers and stepped forth into freedom, not forgetting to kneel down once more on the prison threshold and implore the mercy of Heaven on their persecutors.

The weeks which elapsed before a suitable boat was found for their homeward journey were uncomfortable for the Consul with whom they stayed, and whose wife and servants, they sadly noted, became less and less civil daily. Katherine composed a manifesto and all but smuggled it out of the house; Sarah fasted for a week in sackcloth and commanded the Consul to make God's will known to the Grand Master, to call Malta to repentance. The Consul refused to pass the message on, and when, sure enough, a thunderstorm caused an explosion in the arsenal and a serious fire Sarah could hardly be blamed for recognizing in this the awful consequence of disregarding a heavenly mandate.

In the late summer they were at length taken on board the *Saphire*, Captain Samuel Titswell, who agreed to carry them home. The rest of his passengers were four and twenty Knights of Malta, very fine, aristocratic and condescending. One of them was the Inquisitor's brother and so like him Katherine could have singled him out anywhere. It was, on the contrary, he who singled her out, amused and impressed, perhaps, by the story of her astonishing obstinacy. He led her on to argue, nodded sympathetically and dismissed her with a good-natured platitude: there were many ways to Heaven, he said, but they would all meet there in the end. She had not been three years in prison to let so gross an error pass. 'There is only one way to Heaven', she said tartly.

Their trials were over, but their visions were not. The vessel touched at Tangier, recently handed over to the English by the Portuguese and alive with English troops, whose language and conduct apalled them. They complained to the Governor, and might have preached to the soldiers had their attention not been diverted to the even greater need for redemption of the wild Moorish tribes in the neighbouring hills. Nothing would content them but they must go forth to enlighten the heathen. The Governor curtly refused permission, and the *Saphire* carried the protesting pair rapidly out of the Mediterranean.

Beyond the Pillars of Hercules the story fades away, though now and again across the years their names recur in the long martyrologium of the Quakers, striving as dauntless against the Anglican, as against the Roman, error. It was perhaps Lord d'Aubigny who voiced the respect which transcends doctrine, when in his courtier-priest's rich lodging he received their thanks (for they were grateful). 'Good women,' he said, 'for what service or kindness I have done you, all that I shall desire of you is that when you pray to God, you will remember me in your prayers.' It was the tribute which from time to time the world will pay to Faithful and Valiant for Truth.

CARDINAL RICHELIEU[1]

THE portrait of Richelieu by Philippe de Champaigne, which hangs in the National Gallery, is a striking comment on the greatness of his personality. The narrow, determined chin, the pursed mouth, discriminating and sensual, the observant eyes, and intellectual forehead — here, even to the small pointed beard, was the typical Frenchman of European tradition. There are few clearer proofs of the way in which a dominating personality may set a fashion and establish a mould. How many Mussolinis were not to be met with on a short stroll through any Italian town? English character would not be the same without, say, Queen Elizabeth, Oliver Cromwell or Dr. Johnson. French character and the French nation would have been different without Richelieu.

The great man is known by his legend, and Richelieu has a gigantic legend. It began even before he died, when he travelled France, a sick man, in a litter huge enough to contain himself, his doctors and his secretaries, a litter which was study, office and bedroom in one, and for whose passage the walls of inns had to be knocked down at night-fall. From this lair the 'secret great Cardinal' directed the destinies of the nation which he had made the greatest in Europe. But historic memory is longer and sharper in France than it is here; no French King, who, like Henry VIII, beheaded his wives and bullied his subjects, would have passed into popular tradition as a fiercer Humpty Dumpty and household joke. Nor has Richelieu been mellowed by the passing of three centuries. As the architect of the French monarchy his memory suffered with the spectacular collapse of his work, and thence fell into the hands of the Romantics who made him theatrical, fiendish and sinister. Rescue work by modern historians has not wholly dispelled the cloud.

[1] *Time and Tide*, December 12th, 1942.

The man himself has been obscured by his work, for if his motives are in doubt, his achievements are clear. He made the French monarchy the greatest power in Europe. Heresy and liberty, he used to say, were the two chief enemies, and he dealt with them firmly, almost finally. He broke the Huguenots, disregarded the Estates, started and then controlled the French press, founded the Academy to keep literature in order, and patronized the Sorbonne to do the same for learning; he froze the nobility out of local administration and created a new bureaucracy entirely dependent on the Crown; he dammed up the political aspirations of a vital and intelligent people so formidably that it took them a century and a half to burst the dam. And in Europe he ruthlessly and finally undermined the Habsburg hegemony. Whether these things were to his credit or his discredit depends on how and when you look at them. To-day they are chiefly to his discredit. The man was an early and efficient totalitarian.

But Richelieu differed from the modern dictator in the proportion and sanity of his political perspective. When he said that he hated heresy and liberty, he meant no more than what he said. He did not mean that he hated individuality, enterprise or initiative. He did not regard the State as an end in itself and every man or woman as cogs in the machine. He thought of it as an instrument towards an end, as the mechanism for efficient administration, and no more. It was a harsh view but it was a practical one. Grit clogging the movements of the machine had to be removed; so much the worse if the grit was human. This is a bad principle, but it is a limited one. It leaves, on the whole, great tracts of human activity comparatively free. Moreover, in seventeenth-century France the alternative was political anarchy. It is unfair to condemn Richelieu's solution of the problem of national government because it was not the English one. It could not have been the English one.

The French were not at that time a people with a gift for politics. What they had was a gift for civilization, and what

Richelieu did was to make possible the flowering of that unparalleled genius. Like many great innovators, he did, living, more immediate harm than good. Serving the national interests of France, '*le principe sacré de l'égöisme national*', he laid Germany waste, provoked civil war in Spain, overran Savoy, unleashed murder in the Engadine, sacked Mantua. In order to consolidate an ill-founded Government he tricked and inveigled his opponents to the scaffold, destroyed the innocent with the guilty, jettisoned his assistants and betrayed his friends. Yet on his deathbed, when he was asked to forgive his enemies, he said with perfect sincerity that he had none save the enemies of France. It was true. He was undoubtedly that very questionable thing, a patriot. His ruthless and single-minded work for the French monarchy, his disregard alike of private consciences and private interests, his sweeping away of all, good, bad and indifferent, which stood in the way of the monarchy, made possible the stupendous efflorescence of the French genius, gave to his country that dominating position in the arts of living which she has held through all political vicissitudes for close on three centuries, and which she will surely hold again.

Much of Richelieu's political work is by our standards vicious; much of it is vicious by any standards. Unsound in one particular — he never solved the financial problem — it was bound ultimately to collapse. Nevertheless, he understood, released and guided the essential creative talent of a great people. Man was not made for the State, as he saw it; the State was made for man, and more especially for the French.

He had a curious vanity, a belief that he was a poet. He was never happier, he once astonishingly declared, than when he was writing verses. His career hardly bears out the truth of the assertion, yet the self-deception was typical and significant. Whatever his actions might be, in his heart he knew that the individual creative genius of man was more valuable than the achievements of the statesman.

THE BATTLE OF ROCROI[1]

In the hot August of 1936 I visited the battlefield of Rocroi. Time was short and the autobus service erratic, so that in the end I chugged out from Mézieres in a station taxi. The driver, catching something about a battlefield, was very unwilling to go to Rocroi: there were battlefields of more recent memory closer at hand. If anyone had ever fought at Rocroi, he protested, it was very long ago. Very long ago indeed: on May 19th, 1643.

Three miles on the French side of the Belgian frontier the little eminence of Rocroi dominates the accidented plain with its sparse woods and trickling streams. Within Vauban's massive fortifications, the village seemed grey and wizened, too small for the armour of its mighty prime, and in the grassy dip which once divided the inner from the outer wall, among nettles and food-cans, rusted a roll of wire from a later war. The apathetic girl at the *estaminet* brightened for a moment as she poured out an apéritif; Rocroi, she predicted, would soon be more lively — '*on nous à promis une garnison*'. The shadow of the coming war was the dawn on her horizon.

On the great lichened gate-post an inscription recorded the triumphal entry of the young Condé after his victory over the Spanish army in the plain below. Besieged by the Spaniards in the spring of 1643, Rocroi was relieved in a campaign which settled not only its own fate but that of Spain's power in Europe. About a mile to the south-west of the village, on a slope as innocently green as any in France, marking the centre of the Spanish position stands a small grey monolith: the inadequate gravestone of a nation. Here, backing narrowly line by line under the murderous onslaught of Condé's cavalry, perished the Spanish infantry, the hitherto unbroken shield of that dropsical monarchy whose

[1] *Time and Tide*, May 15th, 1943.

destruction made way for the greatness of France. Here under the green turf their bones still lie — veterans of many campaigns, or young men newly trained to the greatest fighting tradition in Europe: soldiers from Spain and the Spanish provinces, from Castile and Aragon, from the plain of Milan and the uplands of Lombardy (for they were fighters too in those days), from Flanders and Brabant, Luxembourg and Franche Comté, the picked troops, the *Panzerdivisionen* of a great authoritarian Power.

The struggle between the French and Spanish monarchies for the domination of Europe had lasted more than a century before France, emerging from the long night of her religious wars, began under the consolidating genius of Richelieu to gain the advantage. Not that her final victory was sure: far from it. Her armies were still undisciplined, ill-organized, without tradition, and caring more for appearances than war — 'all in bright armour and great feathers, wonderful beautiful to behold'. Only a few years before Richelieu himself had seen Paris nearly taken by a joint attack of the Spaniards with their Austrian and Bavarian allies. When in the spring of 1643 Don Francisco de Melo, Governor of the Spanish Netherlands, invaded France, the outlook for her defenders had seldom been more clouded. Richelieu had died in the preceding winter, and now the King himself lay dying, leaving as his heir a child of five, the future *Roi Soleil*. In command of the army sent to repel the Spanish invasion was the King's cousin, the Duc d'Enghien, a young man of twenty-three. Three older generals had been appointed to control his actions, Senneterre, Gassion and l'Hôpital. But Enghien — who was soon to be known as the great Condé — needed no such control: he was a soldier of genius.

In Paris the King, uneasily dozing on his deathbed among a crowd of courtiers, opened his eyes to see Enghien's father close beside him, and murmured feebly, 'I dreamt your son had won a great victory'. This was on May 13th, a little before he died, and the French army had not as yet engaged the Spanish in the plain below Rocroi.

Don Francisco de Melo was not much perturbed by the approach of the French army. Thinking it better to surround and overwhelm them in their entirety, he had let them advance unmolested through the sparse copses and defile into the open plain. He had the superiority of numbers, though not by so wide a margin as he supposed, for his scouts had been baffled by Enghien's dispositions. When at about six o'clock on the evening of May 18th Senneterre ill-advisedly began the attack, Don Francisco was ready for him, and only the rapid intervention of the young Enghien prevented the destruction of Senneterre's cavalry and enabled the chastened general to extricate his men under cover of night.

The next morning broke fine and warm. On the French side Enghien and Gassion had the right wing. Senneterre and l'Hôpital the left. Facing them, with their backs to the beleaguered fortress, was the Spanish army, cavalry on the wings, infantry and guns in the centre, with German and Flemish reserves in the rear. Enghien's daybreak attack on the opposing cavalry took them by surprise; after a brief resistance they broke and fled. But on the far wing Senneterre was again in trouble. He had the worst of the ground, boggy, and the slope against him. Hard pressed by Melo's superior forces he had all but abandoned the field when Enghien, throwing text-book tactics to the winds, streaked through the centre of the Spanish position, cutting between the Spanish infantry and the reserves, and crashed in on Melo's rear. That finished the Spanish cavalry. Remained the infantry in the centre bereft of all support. They held the position with desperate courage until ammunition began to fail for their twenty-four great cannon and their musketeers. Then the white flag went up. In vain. Enghien advanced to parley, but, mistaking his move for a new attack, someone fired. With cries of *Trahison!* the French surged forward to final and ruthless victory.

Such was the battle of Rocroi, the first laurel wreath to adorn the infant brow of Louis XIV. He had been King for five days.

But laurel wreaths are out of fashion, and it is not for its sake that Rocroi is to be remembered now. Rather because this battle dates — if such things can be exactly dated — the beginning of the long ascendancy of French influence in Europe. There may not have been very much to choose, politically, between the French monarchy and the Spanish; soon those minor Powers who had assisted France to overthrow her rival were leagued as bitterly against France herself. Nor is this surprising, for French Kings fought Spanish Kings not because they disapproved of one Power dominating Europe, but because they wanted themselves to be that Power. International politics, by and large, are a depressing study.

But whatever the political outcome of Rocroi, Europe gained something by that victory which had nothing to do with power politics or rival dynasties, and without which the history of the Continent, even of the world, would have been the poorer. For without the political victory of France the great and vital influence of the most civilized of European peoples would never have achieved its full expansion. Three centuries have passed, and at the close of them the greatest disaster in the recorded history of France. What has become in these last years of the sad girl at the *estaminet*, the garrison which was promised? What strangers have gazed and with what feelings at that lonely monument? Who in France on this 19th of May, 1943, will remember Rocroi? But let us here remember it, not as the first beam of glory from the *Roi Soleil*, but rather as the first ray of that quickening and benevolent sun which, from the genius of the French people, streamed over Europe for close on three centuries, and for lack of which we feel the cold to-day.

I

THE uncouth bulk of Danton gesturing against the dusk and the pungent smell of roast chestnuts from a neighbouring barrow gave for a moment the illusion that nothing had changed. True the arrival, the struggle with luggage among tired crowds in the Metro, had been unlike any previous arrival in Paris, unlike and therefore unevocative, bringing no sudden pain of nostalgia and recognition, like the so often repeated, so familiar panorama of streets slipping past from the taxi window. This time the moment of recognition had been postponed through the sheer physical trouble of arriving and only now as I set down the luggage outside the Odeon station and rested aching arms in the half darkness, the full flood of recognition came.

The eye travels — at home and delighted — over the high outline of the houses dwindling away down the Boulevard St. Germain, the yellow pools of street lamps in the dusk, the familiar clefts which the brain seeks to identify, Rue de la Seine, Rue de l'Ecole de Médecine . . .; delighted with the hurrying crowds, the fire-lit group round the chestnut seller, the shawled newswomen yelling rhythmically . . . The ear detects the first evident change, for that 'Paris-Soir', that 'Ami du Peuple' which were so much a part of the oral pattern of a Paris evening have gone. They are calling strange names with as yet no associations. The ear misses in another second the clang of the trams, the whistle of the police, the discordant stridency of Paris traffic. Only a few cars devour at terrifying speed the slithering distance of the street.

It was, doubtless, sentimental, but I had not wanted for the first hours at least to see anyone I knew or had known; I had come first to see Paris, and cities are to a great extent what a personal

[1] *Time and Tide*, January 12th, 19th, 26th, 1946.

memory has made of them. So that it was after all a purely
sentimental, even an egoist approach, a desire to awaken recollec-
tions, to renew sensations half-remembered, a desire to find out as
much what had become of that ingenuous and dogmatic student
who so many years before had experienced in these streets the
simultaneous discovery of Cartesianism and first love as to find
out what had become of Paris.

Turning away from Danton I missed a familiar frock-coated
figure on the neighbouring plinth. The plinth was still there,
plastered with political notices, but its occupant had gone. He
was not, I was to learn within the next twenty-four hours, the
only one. Chiappe with his telegraph at the foot of Raspail, the
two old doctors in the Avenue de l'Observatoire, Shakespeare in
the Boulevard Haussman, Etienne Dolet (here even the bronze
plaques which surrounded his pedestal are chiselled away) all had
gone to feed Germany's hunger for metal; only a few have been
spared – Henri Quatre, Joan of Arc, La Fayette brandishing his
outsize sword. Not perhaps a very serious artistic loss but forgotten worthies are a part of the natural accumulation of a great
city and their departure leaves a scar. Besides we shall surely never
again live through a period so prone to statues as the last century
and this peculiar form of urban embellishment has already a
period charm it is sad to lose.

The cold and sunlight of the next morning imposed an air of
immobility on the scene. The criss-crossed perspectives of the
bare Luxembourg trees were deserted; the tracery of frosted
branches, the stone princesses vigilant over the gravel paths, and
the fountains garlanded with ice were like the drop scene for a
ballet. Even the ranks of frozen cabbages where once had been
flower beds and stretches of lawn gave no sense of reality. This
scenic Paris unfolded itself in the sharp light unaltered, beautiful,
and yet – for me at least on that day, by some trick of the intense
cold – washed clean of contents, a vessel of which the life seemed
for the moment stilled, waiting for the new impulse which would

set all going again. An illusion of course. How could it truly be so
in a city of immense, continuous, vigorous life? Yet there is undoubtedly — as I came to notice later when I talked with friends —
a sense of expectancy, of transition. The Fourth Republic is still
to make. The new period of Paris and of France has not yet
begun. For all the enthusiasm and excitement which renewed
contact with French culture has provoked here in England, the
frozen fountains have hardly yet begun to thaw.

Along the Seine the bouquinistes were not yet at their places
but the sight of their green boxes clamped to the embankment
wall was reassuring. The central doorway of Notre-Dame was
black-draped for the inevitable funeral. Inside it seemed loftier,
darker, grimmer than I remembered. There was a chill almost of
Puritanism in the air. In the south transept a gaunt cross of wood,
towering, narrow, to the height of the clerestory windows and
sombrely draped with the tricolour, commanded attention. This
cross, I read, was shortly to go to Buchenwald to mark the
resting-place of the French dead.

Moving further, towards the holy murmur and the gentle glow
which was coming from the Lady Chapel, I realized with a sudden
shock what it was that gave so gaunt an air to the great church —
that same coldness that I had noticed and again failed to identify in
a brief visit to Saint Germain des Prés in the darkness of the
previous evening. There are no candles to be had in Paris. In a
straightforward sense, and without double meaning, the lights
had been put out.

It is something — indeed it is much — that among the ruins of
Europe Paris has survived almost intact. There are scars but not
irreparable ones from the days of that glorious August which
added another astounding chapter to the fierce record of the
city. It is commemorated more tragically in the innumerable
simple stone tablets which at one strategic street corner after
another record the names of those killed in the fight for the
liberation. Some had pots or vases of flowers beneath them, dead

in the wintry wind, almost all had tricolour favours, frayed and discoloured, fixed to the stone. 'Ces pauvres petits du F.F.I. . . .' a woman sighed; it was indeed the word. 'Agé de 20 ans . . . agé de 18 ans . . . agé de 21 ans . . .' in monotonous succession, 'morts pour la France'. Not in vain . . . ? I wondered, considering the immense drabness of the European scene, and this strangely unfamiliar city, this recognizable structure of which the life had so deeply altered. But remember their ages once again; these young men had not died for the Paris or the France which I knew. They had died, and that is the secret, for a new France. Many were too young to have died for anything else.

II

It is an easy mistake, and one often made by the English observer, to take the trappings of France for the heart of France, and to think that the effervescence and vitality which used to be the most immediately striking characteristic of the French scene was also the most essential. There is an underlying hardness, a disciplined and determined strength at the heart of the French character. A certain Puritanism is a persistent and emphatic theme in their history, and an important part of their contribution to the civilization of Western Europe. We forget too often that a ferment as fundamental and as widespread as that of the Revolution came two centuries earlier out of France in the name of John Calvin. But quite apart from the importance of the Huguenot tradition — it played and still plays a part comparable to the Non-conformist tradition here — in French history itself, the harsh fighting strength of Protestantism in Western Europe was the creation of a Frenchman. Moreover, there is a highly Puritan strain which recurs time and again in French Catholic thought, from the founders of Cluny and Citeaux to the Trappists.

Discipline and austerity can be an expression as eloquent and natural to the French as the colour, the *faste*, the subtlety and the vitality, which are more obviously connected with the French tradition. It is to those depths of the national character that the France of to-day seems to have returned, to a fundamental seriousness of purpose; impossible to avoid the idea that the four years' ordeal has effected an immense purification.

Faced by a Paris grown grey and hard it is difficult at first to find the new bearings. The long tumultous history of France — yet a history which has been notably consistent in the reiterant rhythm of its inconsistencies — provides explanations which we should not neglect in analysing the elements of a country which years of separation and a measure of experience wholly different from our own has made unfamiliar.

> L'obscurité couvre le monde,
> Mais l'Idée illumine et luit;
> De sa clarté blanche elle inonde
> Les sombres azurs de la nuit. . . .

thus Victor Hugo from his place of exile. *L'Idée* is perhaps the most important force in the history of France; but there have been too many of them. The French mind, riotously fertile in theory, and the French brain, vigorously active in practice, have clothed too many ideas with the flesh of practical politics for the tranquillity of their own country. Not here the blinkered forward stumble of the English down what has been on the whole a single political track. France has demonstrated to Europe, Empire and Commune, absolute Monarchy and Revolution. The fruitfulness in theory and the experiments in practice leave behind them a trail of antagonisms: inevitable penalty of having too many ideas and too much skill and passion in carrying them out.

Yet ultimately the idea of France itself overshadows all the others. Conceptions of nationality have, unhappily, no decisive outline. *La France*, to each man or woman who died for her, meant something different — the landscape of home, a symbolic

figure, a political concept in action, a vision, a recollection or a
hope. Those who told us what they felt before they died tell us
little — and much. 'Je suis mort pour une image plus belle que
celles que je voyais depuis la défaite . . .' 'Je meurs pour mon
pays et pour mon Dieu . . .' 'Je ne meurs ni pour une faction, ni
pour un homme. Je meurs pour Elle, pour mon idée à moi de la
servir . . .' Deeply moving these last letters, perhaps most of all in
that final inarticulacy. The idea is still an idea uncorrupted by
practice, unconfined by definition. Over what gulfs of misunderstanding, what differences of heritage and outlook this one
luminous idea cast a cloak of heroic sameness; over the Left and
the Right, the Monarchist and the Communist, the disreputable
and the respectable.

If never before in the history of France has so great a disaster
come upon the nation, not for centuries has come so great an opportunity. But the faith in France which originated and upheld
the Resistance becomes inevitably confused in the practice of
quotidian politics, and the contradictory elements which made up
the Resistance had split into their component parts before the
first winter of liberation.

III

The austerity and self-discipline, which are profound elements
in the French tradition, should not be underestimated; but neither
must it be forgotten that the major problem of France, during a
vigorous and fruitful history, has been the excess of ideas. From
the combination of these two qualities — mental discipline and
mental fertility — comes the greatness of the French contribution
to civilization as well as most of the evils of French history. Thus
the combination at a single moment of extreme fertility of ideas
with a renewed discipline may be in the highest degree fortunate
— or disastrous. So much depends on the nature of the ideas which

are in the ascendant and the form which the new austerity takes.

What is disturbing in France to-day is the dominance, especially among the young, of the belief that creative activity in the arts must be relevant to the political conflict of the time. I cannot believe that among a people so profoundly sane and civilized as the French this deforming Germanic doctrine will long prevail. Its influence there, and to a considerable extent here also, is the inevitable legacy of the struggle against Germany. In order to overthrow the enemy it has been necessary — as it always is — to fight him with his own weapons and to assimilate in part the very ideas against which the struggle was being waged.

It would, of course, be flying in the face of history to suggest that the subjection of all activity to political standards is an idea foreign to the French. It was, after all, in France that the theory of the all-controlling State was first most effectively put into practice and it is in the French dictionary that the word *étatisme* makes its first appearance. The fruitfulness of French theories has this result — that few if any political concepts are wholly foreign to her. The return, therefore, of ideas which since they left French soil have passed through German, or for that matter Russian, transformations, is doubly dangerous. They link themselves too easily to elements which already exist in the multitudinous French tradition.

All the more to be regretted therefore, at a time when the discipline of the State is everywhere increasing, is the prevalence in France of the belief that creative art should be 'engaged'. For the independence of the artist is one of the great safeguards of the freedom of the human spirit.

More immediately serious for the political future of France — since the artist in the long run can be trusted to emancipate himself — is the close and conscious disciplining of parties. *La vie Parlementaire est bien malade*, a French statesman regretfully told me; it needed no very perceptive eye to see the truth of this. The fight for life, from which France has barely emerged, imposed a war discipline on the new forces in French politics and impregnated the younger generation with an attitude to politics which is not only profoundly serious — an excellent thing — but carries in its discipline and rigour the marks of its fighting origin.

To say that France to-day faces once more the problem of deciding the place of the individual in the State, is to say only that France is facing the eternal problem of politics, the problem which confronts us all. For eighteen months, since before the liberation until almost the end of 1945, Jean Anouilh's adaptation of *Antigone* was to be seen at the little *Atelier*. No play based on that original could be devoid of greatness and the moment could hardly have been more apt. The play, which was passed by the German censor, handles the theme of the individual in revolt against authority with so delicate a balance that the sympathetic treatment of Antigone gave secret pleasure before the liberation and the sympathetic treatment of Creon has caused some annoyance since.

M. Anouilh's version, played in modern dress, brings language and allusions up to date and here and there comes near the danger of sentimentalizing the details; but the acid sharpness of the great original is preserved. Antigone remains unreasonable, obstinate and a nuisance, the small rock on which the State splits. Even the reiterated reference to her as *la petite Antigone* makes her more, rather than less, exasperating. *Sans la petite Antigone nous aurions tous vécus bien tranquilles* . . . the chorus, suave in dress suit, concludes the tragedy and we are left to think the rest out for ourselves.

It is not good, and fortunately it is not possible, that we should all live *bien tranquilles*. When the State manages so to constitute itself as to liquidate all its Antigones, not after but *before* they can assert their intolerable and intolerant independence, there will be a great desolation of the human spirit. Against the German menace it was, in the last resort, *la petite Antigone* who revolted. It was not, of course, *la petite Antigone* who won, because discipline and organization are necessary in order to overthrow discipline and organization. But it will be a sad day for France and for the world if the society which was reborn in the collapse of Germany has no room for its Antigones.

THE HISTORIAN AND THE WORLD[1]

THE historian has much to answer for. History – that is, written history – has made and unmade States, given courage to the oppressed and undermined the oppressor, has justified aggression and over-ridden law. A French historian, in the cruel light of 1870, exclaimed with unwilling admiration that the Germans used their history as a means towards unity and a weapon of war; but the story of his own country as written by his compatriots had taught the French people, he lamented, 'surtout de häir les uns les autres'. Past glories have inspired whole nations to rise again, as witness the Risorgimento, as witness Poland and Bohemia. Past heroism breeds future heroism, past cowardice the cowardice of the future. Within the limits of the modern nation, history tends to repeat itself by a process of almost deliberate imitation. We know what to expect of ourselves and, by expecting, do it.

But what is this force? What is written history? Froude sonorously hailed it as 'a voice forever sounding across the centuries the laws of right and wrong', and thereby summed up a general if an unconscious belief. Written history is, in fact, nothing of the kind; it is the fragmentary record of the often inexplicable actions of innumerable bewildered human beings, set down and interpreted according to their own limitations by other human beings, equally bewildered. The tribunal of history judges about as fairly as an average bench of magistrates; which is exactly what it is. But only a minority of people are able to recognize this fact, and, of that minority, only a minority will act upon it. The rest of us will go through life with a silt of moral and political prejudice washing about in the brain which has been derived directly and indirectly, by way of text-book and propaganda, school and home and theatre and market-place, from

1 *Time and Tide*, November 14th and 21st, 1942.

historical writings. For, somewhere about the eighteenth century, history tacitly replaced religion as the school of public morals. 'Standard works' instead of volumes of sermons appeared in every gentleman's library. History was promoted from being entertainment to being the most frequent form of serious reading. Nothing has yet taken its place.

Whatever the faults of the priests and preachers and theologians who were indirectly responsible for the deplorable state of things in Medieval and Renaissance Europe, they knew what their function was, even if they failed to perform it. Moreover, they enjoyed full public recognition. Their successors, the historians, enjoy no such recognition and the best men among them have often been unaware of their influence, or afraid to use it.

There are two kinds of writer concerned with history: the scholars and the popularizers. The scholars spend their time excavating small fragments of the past which, once disinterred and the dust blown off, they present, like Shelley's nosegay — O! to whom? To the second kind of writer, the popularizer; and a popularizer may be anyone from an upright and learned man to Dr. Goebbels: but usually he is Dr. Goebbels. It is not for the scholars, burrowing with their noses deep in the past and their eyes dimmed to the pale light of the archives, to notice who is making use of the material they industriously scratch up. Nor is it for them to give any guidance as to how it is to be used. They are no more concerned with the ultimate outcome of their studies than is the research-scientist with the use of poison gas in warfare. The final results arise not from the nature of the material but from the depravity of human beings; and historical research of the truly scholastic kind is not connected with human beings at all. It is a pure study, like higher mathematics.

Very different is the position of the popularizers. They have to use, digest, and re-deliver the material in a form palatable to the public; their business is essentially with human beings, both the living and the dead. Some of them have no conscious idea beyond that of writing a readable book; others have a very definite idea of teaching a political or moral lesson through their book. In both these groups there are good men and learned men; in both these groups there are charlatans. But as far as the world is concerned only the learning and the goodness, only the vices and the charlatanism of the second group have borne fruit. For the work of those who have no message beyond the mere reconstruction of the past is sterile.

It used to be said that history should be written without prejudice: that the historian must not step aside to draw a moral. The first cannot be done; the second should not. Historians should always draw morals. If the accurate, judicious and highly trained fail to do so, the unscrupulous and unqualified will do it for them, and the deluded public will listen gaping to false but more emphatic prophets. It is futile for the upright man to say, 'I have set down nothing in malice, I have made no unsound deductions. I have neither omitted nor strained a record', unless he can add — 'And I have written a book far more persuasive than anything of Rosenberg's and as many people have read it'. The historian who neglects the education of his public is as much responsible for the villainous stuff to which they go instead, as Gallio was for the disgraceful exhibition which took place in his court of justice. A nation does not create the historians it deserves; the historians are far more likely to create the nation.

Over the last century more and more people have become literate; more and more people have become (or until recently had become) vocal members of their community or State. The position of the writer became correspondingly more influential and more responsible. This was not the moment for him to go off into abstruse mumblings about art for art's sake. The artist at all times has a duty towards society; let him outrage it, by all means, for its own good, but — with rare exceptions — he must not retire from it into the private circle of his own artistic integrity. Of all writers this is truest of the historians who have, willy nilly, been pushed by sociological and spiritual forces outside their control into the position of chief exponents of political morality.

It is a part which all but a few historians have been lamentably unable to play. There have been exceptions: Mommsen, unfortunately, because his message, conveyed through a learned history of Rome, was the worship of force; Macaulay, fortunately, because his message, conveyed through a less learned history of England, was the worship of liberal institutions and free will. 'Four hundred editions', thundered Carlyle, incensed at the levity of its style, 'could not lend it any permanent value.' He failed to see that four hundred editions in themselves may well constitute a permanent value; his attack was based on the groundless faith that there is an absolute standard outside the praise and agreement of the public. For the historian there is not.

Macaulay may have been inaccurate and biased; but he preached a good cause eloquently. There has been a fashion for sneering at his errors, but his ghost has the laugh of us for we are all the heirs of his stalwart prejudices. If we believe ourselves to be a great democratic nation, if we believe in a broadening tradition of liberty, we believe it to a great extent because Macaulay wrote history in a manner which conquered generations of readers and filtered through text-books and the schools to become part of the common conviction of a whole people.

But the greater number of historical writers failed entirely to understand what was expected of them. They turned their faces away from their audience and towards their subject, turned deliberately from the present to the past. They began to consider with misguided conscientiousness their duty to the dead. This was nonsense, for no one has a duty to the dead except in relation to the living. The misinterpretation of a dead man causes him no discomfort though it may radically affect the lessons which posterity learns from his career. The Nazis were concerned not with the ghost of Frederick the Great but with the minds of the Hitler Jugend, when they made the traducing of German national figures a punishable offence. By 'traducing' they meant disturbing the layer of accepted prejudice in the minds of the people.

Misinterpretation of past ages is more or less inevitable, and, although a respect for truth is an essential quality for the good historian, his understanding will always be limited by individual peculiarities. That is why it is important, if his style is persuasive and his learning impressive, that he should also be a good man. The dead can look after themselves; the living cannot.

The historian's first duty is not to his subject, but to his audience — not that he should tamper with truth as he sees it, but he should write nothing without considering the weakness, prejudice and ignorance with which he is surrounded and in which he shares; and considering too the prophetic and didactic part which has been forced upon him. It is as important for the historian to-day to be a good, and if possible a great, man as it was for the high dignitaries of the Medieval Church. It is all too easy, armed with this romantic, this most appealing of weapons, to play unfairly on the wishful thoughts of the ingenuous. 'We see those splendid barbarians', wrote Houston Stewart Chamberlain in an outburst of imaginative word painting, 'glowing with youth, free, making their entry into history endowed with all those qualities which fit them for the very highest place.' In this flattering mirror of their ancestors, thousands of swarthy and mouse-coloured nonentities, tightly buttoned into frockcoats, at once recognized themselves. Alas, with what results . . . Chamberlain was no scholar and his barbarians were the figment of his imagination; but fine scholarship will not save the historian from perpetrating such crimes. Mommsen and Treitschke were great scholars, but when they came to interpret their material they believed that might was right, and all their knowledge served but to poison the minds of their compatriots.

Gabriel Hanotaux, the veteran French historian, spoke as a

young man of 'la courbe magnifique de l'histoire *agie*, s'insérant dans l'histoire écrite'. But this, too, is a reversal of what happens, for there is no process by which the cross-hatched complexity of acted history can be reproduced faithfully in the written word. Yet the word effectively written will reproduce itself with uncanny truth in the acts of the future.

What is the solution? There is none that can be called satisfactory, for bad men will continue to be popular writers and may even, in the technical sense, be 'good' historians. The high-minded and the morally responsible will never have the monopoly of the historian's profession or of the public ear; but they should at least recognize what is expected of them and sustain on equal terms their fight for a hearing.